FEB 17 1995

LIBERACE

LIVES OF NOTABLE GAY MEN AND LESBIANS

LIBERACE

RAY MUNGO

MARTIN DUBERMAN, General Editor

CHELSEA HOUSE PUBLISHERS ■ New York • Philadelphia

CHELSEA HOUSE PUBLISHERS

EDITORIAL DIRECTOR   Richard Rennert
EXECUTIVE MANAGING EDITOR   Karyn Gullen Browne
COPY CHIEF   Robin James
PICTURE EDITOR   Adrian G. Allen
ART DIRECTOR   Robert Mitchell
MANUFACTURING DIRECTOR   Gerald Levine
ASSISTANT ART DIRECTOR   Joan Ferrigno

LIVES OF NOTABLE GAY MEN AND LESBIANS
SENIOR EDITOR   Sean Dolan
SERIES DESIGN   Basia Niemczyc

Staff for **LIBERACE**
ASSISTANT EDITORS   Annie McDonnell, Mary B. Sisson
PICTURE RESEARCHER   Patricia Burns
COVER ILLUSTRATION   Bonnie T. Gardner

Introduction © 1994 by Martin B. Duberman.

First Printing

1   3   5   7   9   8   6   4   2

Library of Congress Cataloging-in-Publication Data

Mungo, Raymond, 1946–
Liberace/Ray Mungo.
p. cm.—(Lives of notable gay men and lesbians)
Includes bibliographical references and index.
ISBN 0-7910-2850-X.
     0-7910-2885-2 (pbk.)
1. Liberace, 1919– —Juvenile literature. 2. Pianists—United States—Biography—Juvenile literature. 3. Gay men—United States—Biography—Juvenile literature. [1. Liberace, 1919– . 2. Pianists. 3. Musicians. 4. Gay men—Biography.] I. Title. II. Series: Lives of notable gay men and lesbians.
ML3930.L45M86 1994   94-10201
786.2'092—dc20   CIP
[B]   AC MN

CONTENTS

Titles in
▣ LIVES OF NOTABLE GAY MEN AND LESBIANS ▣

GAY, STRAIGHT, AND IN BETWEEN

Martin Duberman

Being different is never easy. Especially in a culture like ours, which puts a premium on conformity and equates difference with deficiency. And especially during the teenage years when one feels desperate for acceptance and vulnerable to judgment. If you are taller or shorter than average, or fatter or thinner, or physically challenged, or of the "wrong" color, gender, religion, nationality, or sexual orientation, you are likely to be treated as "less than," as inferior to what the majority has decreed is the optimal, standard model.

Theoretically, those of us who are different should be delighted that we are *not* ordinary, not just another cookie-cutter product of mainstream culture. We should glory in the knowledge that many remarkably creative figures, past and present, lived outside accepted norms and pressed hard against accepted boundaries.

But in reality many of us have internalized the majority's standards of worth, and we do not feel very good about ourselves. How could we?

When we look around us, we see that most people in high places of visibility, privilege, and power are white, heterosexual males of a very traditional kind. That remains true even though intolerance may have ebbed *somewhat* in recent decades and people of diverse backgrounds may have *begun* to attain more of a foothold in our culture.

Many gay men and lesbians through time have looked and acted like "ordinary" people and could therefore choose to "stay in the closet" and avoid social condemnation—though the effort at concealment produced its own turmoil and usually came at the price of self-acceptance. On the other hand, "sissy" gay men or "butch" lesbians have been quickly categorized and scorned by the mainstream culture as "sexual deviants"—even though no necessary link exists between gender nonconformity and sexual orientation. In the last 15 years or so, however, more and more people who previously would have passed as straight *have* been choosing to "come out." They sense that social consequences are no longer as severe as they once were—and that the psychic costs of concealment are taking too great a toll.

Yet even today, there are comparatively few role models available for gays and lesbians to emulate. And unlike other oppressed minorities, homosexuals don't often find confirmation within their own families. Even when a homosexual child is not rejected outright, acceptance comes within a family unit that is structurally heterosexual and in which homosexuality is generally mocked and decried. With his or her different desire and experience, the gay son or lesbian daughter remains an exotic. Moreover, such children are unable to find in family lore and traditions—as other minority people can—a compensatory source of validation to counterbalance the ridicule of mainstream culture.

Things are rarely any better at school, where textbooks and lessons are usually devoid of relevant information about homosexuality. Nor does the mainstream culture—movies or television, for example—often provide gays or lesbians with positive images of themselves, let alone any sense of historical antecedents. These silences are in large measure a reflection of the culture's homophobia. But to a lesser degree they reflect two other matters as well: the fact that many accomplished gay men and lesbians in the past refused to publicly acknowledge their sexuality (sometimes even to themselves); and secondly, the problem of assigning "gay" or "lesbian" identities to past figures who lived at a time when those conceptual categories did not exist.

For the surprising finding of recent scholarship is that categorizing human beings on the basis of sexual desire alone is a relatively recent phenomenon of the last several hundred years. It is a development, many historians believe, tied to the increasing urbanization of Europe and the Americas, and to the new opportunities city life presented for anonymity—for freedom from the relentless scrutiny of family and neighbors that had characterized farming communities and small towns. Only with the new freedom afforded by city life, historians are telling us, could people who felt they were different give free rein to their natures, lay claim to a distinctive identity, and begin to elaborate a subculture that would reflect it.

Prior to, say, 1700 (the precise date is under debate), the descriptive categories of "straight" or "gay" were not widely employed in dividing up human nature. Even today, in many non-Western parts of the world, it is unusual to categorize people on the basis of sexual orientation alone. Through time and across cultures it has often been assumed that *both* same- and opposite-gender erotic feelings (what we now call "bisexuality") could coexist in an individual—even if *acting* on same-gender impulses was usually taboo.

In the West, where we *do* currently divide humanity into oppositional categories of "gay" and "straight," most people grow up accepting that division as "natural" and dutifully assign themselves to one category or the other. Those who adopt the definition "gay" or "lesbian," however, soon discover that mainstream culture offers homosexuals (unlike heterosexuals) no history or sense of forebears. This is a terrible burden, especially during the teenage years, when one is actively searching for a usable identity, for a continuum in which to place oneself and lay claim to a contented and productive life.

This series is designed, above all, to fill that huge, painful cultural gap. It is designed to instill not only pride in antecedents but encouragement, the kind of encouragement that literature and biography have always provided: proof that someone else out there has felt what we have felt,

9

experienced what we have experienced, been where we have been—and has endured, achieved, and flourished.

But *who* to include in this series has been problematic. Even today, many people refuse to define themselves as gay or lesbian. In some cases, they do not wish to confine what they view as their fluid sexuality into narrow, either/or categories. In other cases, they may acknowledge to themselves that their sexuality does fit squarely within the "gay" category, yet refuse to say so publicly, unwilling to take on the onus of a lesbian or gay identity. In still other cases, an individual's sense of sexual identity can change during his or her lifetime, as can his or her sense of its importance, when compared with many other strands, in defining their overall temperament.

Complicating matters still further is the fact that even today—when multitudes openly call themselves gay or lesbian, and when society as a whole argues about gay marriage and parenting or the place of gay people in the military—there is still no agreed-upon definition of what centrally constitutes a gay or lesbian identity. Should we call someone gay if his or her sexual desire is *predominantly* directed toward people of their own gender? But then how do we establish predominance? And by "desire" do we mean actual behavior—or fantasies that are never acted out? (Thus Father John McNeill, the writer and Jesuit, has insisted—though he has never actually had sex with another man—that on the basis of his erotic fantasies, he *is* a gay man.)

Some scholars and theorists even argue that genital sexuality need not be present in a relationship before we can legitimately call it gay or lesbian, stressing instead the central importance of same-gender *emotional* commitment. The problem of definition is then further complicated when we include the element of *self*-definition. If we come across someone in the past who does not explicitly self-identify as gay, by what right, and according to what evidence, can we claim them anyway?

Should we eliminate all historical figures who lived before "gay" or "lesbian" were available categories for understanding and ordering their experience? Are we entitled, for the purposes of this series, to include at least some of those from the past whose sexuality seems not to have been confined to one gender or the other, or who—as a cover, to protect a public image or a career—may have married, and thus have been commonly taken to be heterosexual? And if we do not include some of those whose sexuality cannot be clearly categorized as "gay," then how can we speak of a gay and lesbian continuum, a *history*?

In deciding which individuals to include in *Notable Gay Men and Lesbians,* I have gone back and forth between these competing definitions, juggling, combining, and, occasionally, finessing them. For the most part, I have tried to confine my choices to those figures who *by any definition* (same-gender emotional commitment, erotic fantasy, sexual behavior, *and* self-definition) do clearly qualify for inclusion.

But alas, we often lack the needed intimate evidence for such clear-cut judgments. I have regretfully omitted from the series many bisexual figures, and especially the many well-known women—Tallulah Bankhead, Judy Garland, Greta Garbo, or Josephine Baker, for example—whose erotic and emotional preference seem indeterminable (usually for lack of documentation). But I will probably also include a few—Margaret Mead, say, or Marlene Dietrich—as witnesses to the difficult ambiguities of sexual definition, and to allow for a discussion of those ambiguities.

In any case, I suspect much of the likely criticism over this or that choice will come from those eager to conceal their distaste for a series devoted to "Notable (no less!) Gay Men and Lesbians" under the guise of protesting a single inclusion or omission within it. That kind of criticism can be easily borne, and is more than compensated for, by the satisfaction of acquainting today's young gays and lesbians—and indeed all who feel "different"—with knowledge of some of those distinguished forebears whose existence can inform and comfort them.

❖   ❖   ❖

Liberace may seem a curious choice for a book series entitled *Notable Gay Men and Lesbians.* Some would say he was "notable" only for having been notoriously extravagant and flamboyant—not for having been singularly gifted nor for having left behind a prodigious body of work.

And as for claiming Liberace as a "gay man," did he not publicly and insistently deny for most of his life that he *was* homosexual?

It needs to be said, first of all, that this series is not reserved only for exemplary lives—for paragons of virtue or of inexhaustible accomplishment. On the grounds of his fame alone, however transient it may prove, Liberace's inclusion in this series might be justified. At one point in his career, he was the highest-paid entertainer in the world, and decidedly a show business legend. Moreover, as Ray Mungo writes in this engaging, compassionate biography of Mr. Showmanship, Liberace "was something special, someone unique, a self-created entity, an amazing, blazing sensation."

On a broader level still, Liberace's life tells us much about what traits our culture will or will not reward, and also much about the distortions of personality that follow the quest for public notoriety. None of the people written about in this series had a wholly admirable character, or relationships that were uniformly harmonious, or an integrity not somewhat compromised by ambition. Perfect role models can be found only in the world of fairytale fantasy, not in the conflicted everyday world the rest of us inhabit.

It could be argued that Liberace's character, relationships, and integrity were seriously flawed—but then so was the world that formed him. In the 1950s, when Liberace was achieving fame, the psychiatric profession was all but unanimous in declaring homosexuality an "illness." Senator Joseph McCarthy and J. Edgar Hoover, the head of the F.B.I., had inaugurated something like a reign of terror in their efforts to uncover and destroy nonconformists of all kinds. (McCarthy, interestingly, has long been rumored to have been a repressed gay man, and J. Edgar Hoover lived in a domestic arrangement for decades with Clyde Tolson, another high-ranking F.B.I. official.)

Very few gays and lesbians dared to "come out" publicly in those pre-Stonewall years. A few hundred brave souls did band together politically, but their activities were often clandestine and necessarily timid. For an entertainer like Liberace, with a large, adoring female following, the revelation of homosexuality would have seriously threatened and possibly destroyed his career. To survive, he had to live a double life, keeping his sexual trysts and love affairs with men secret. Even so, the rumors spread, and only Liberace's brazen denials (and the sloppy research of the press) kept the rumors from being confirmed as truth.

That kind of insistent denial takes its toll. Double-dealing becomes a way of life, disguise, second nature. And in recounting the terrible psychic costs of staying in the closet to Liberace himself, Ray Mungo has given us an additional and most important reason for including his story in this series; namely, to show the debilitating effects of furtiveness and deceit. Liberace lived lavishly, but not contentedly. He had a large amount of sex over his lifetime, but very little love. No matter how many shopping sprees he went on, he could not cover over the emptiness within. Nor could any amount of plastic surgery conceal his internal scars.

The engine driving this disconsolate life—and on this point we must be clear and emphatic—was not some fatal flaw Liberace had been born with, but rather the self-hatred which a homophobic society engendered within him. Lying and evasion were strategies for survival. Had Liberace dared to be more open and unapologetic about who he really was, he would almost surely have never achieved or would quickly have lost his legendary status as Mr. Showmanship. Liberace was not that kind of moral hero. He mirrored the world which shaped him. He could not rise above it. ▩

CHAPTER ONE

BOY WONDER
OF THE IVORIES

*"With a name like Liberace, which stands for freedom,
I'm for anything that has the letters L-I-B in it, and that
includes Gay Lib."*

—Liberace, 1986

He was the most famous piano player of the 20th century, surpassing even great concert pianists like Horowitz and Paderewski. Loved by millions, he was the highest-paid entertainer in the world and the first matinee idol created by TV. He was outrageous and flamboyant, known for his mind-boggling wardrobe and trademark candelabra.

He was the one and only Liberace (pronounced Li-ber-AH-chee), and he was gay. At the age of 10 he had realized that he was sexually attracted to men. Later in life, he was attracted to teenage boys on whom he lavished cars, gifts, jewelry, and money. But he refused to admit to being gay for fear it would wreck his fabulous career, remaining stubbornly in the closet until his death from AIDS on February 4, 1987, in Palm Springs, California.

Liberace and a friend take a dip in the pool of one of his many houses. Known for his extravagance both on and off the stage, Liberace nonetheless carefully controlled his image, shielding his homosexuality from the public eye.

15

Colorful and talented in public, wild and extravagant in private, Liberace was yet deeply conservative in his willingness to live a double life. The onstage Liberace was a show business legend, universally known as Mr. Showmanship and adored by legions of older women. The offstage Liberace was a homosexual flirting with disaster, hosting all-male parties around his pool, keeping young male lovers, yet suing anyone who dared to publicly label him as gay.

In his first two years on television (1952–54), he made $7 million—an unthinkably huge sum for that time. For the last 25 years of his life, he earned an average of $5 million annually, allowing him to support his large entourage of employees, live-in boyfriends, and wardrobe designers. He maintained lavish, sprawling homes in Las Vegas, Palm Springs, and Los Angeles and owned numerous customized automobiles, staggering amounts of flashy jewelry, and a large collection of all-male pornography. He spent his money as fast as it came in, leaving behind an estate that consisted of a lot of property but not much cash.

Liberace may not live long in musical history. He was neither a classical musician nor a pop music star. He was, simply put, *Liberace,* something special, someone unique, a self-created entity, an amazing, blazing sensation. "When You're Hot, You're Hot!" the marquee always proclaimed for his Las Vegas engagements. "Too much of a good thing is *wonderful!*" was his oft-proclaimed philosophy of life. His theme song, which he played at the end of every concert, was "I'll Be Seeing You (In All the Old Familiar Places)."

The life of Liberace began humbly on May 16, 1919, in West Allis, Wisconsin, a suburb of Milwaukee. Wladziu Valentino Liberace, who had a twin brother who died at birth, entered the world weighing 13 pounds. "He took all the strength from his little brother," his mother, Frances Zuchowski, the daughter of Polish immigrants, later said. "That was a sign." His father, Salvatore Liberace, known as Sam, was himself an immigrant, from Formia, Italy. Wladziu was a Polish name, equivalent to Walter, while Valentino was a tribute to Rudolph Valentino, the great Italian-American silent film idol, his mother's favorite actor. The young Liberace, who was called Wally by family and friends, was one of four surviving children: George was eight years older; Ange-

Born of a musical family,

Lee's talents are natural.

But they might never

have matured had not his family

loved and encouraged him.

Liberace's parents, Frances Zuchowski (right) and Salvatore "Sam" Liberace, were both musically inclined. However, Sam's career as a French horn player was never successful enough to support his large family.

lina, five years older; and Rudy, also named after Valentino, was ten years younger.

Young Wally's parents had met at a concert given by the famous John Philip Sousa marching band in Menasha, Wisconsin. Sam Liberace was a French horn player in the Sousa outfit. After their marriage, the couple lived in Philadelphia, Pennsylvania, for a short while, but

Frances hated the big city and persuaded Sam to move back to Wisconsin, where her parents had a farm between Menasha and Neenah.

Sam Liberace was a serious, dedicated musician who longed to see his children become accomplished musicians, but as there was not much work for French horn players in small-town Wisconsin, especially during the Great Depression of the 1930s, he was often unemployed, which led to much domestic unhappiness and turmoil. For several years, the family operated a small grocery store and lived in the apartment behind it, an arrangement that Liberace, who hated the shabbiness of his parents' home and the constant fighting and bickering that went on there, later remembered as humiliating and demeaning. He often sought escape on his grandparents' farm. With most of the necessities of life—food, money, clothing—in short supply in the household, the Liberace kids constantly competed with each other, but when it came to his mother's affection, Wally was always the winner. Her clear favorite, he was showered with attention.

One of the things the children competed for was time on the family piano in the parlor. While George took up the violin, both Wally and Angie studied the piano, and initially they had to share time practicing on the old upright. But in a short time this, too, proved no contest. It became apparent that while Angie was a competent player, Wally was a true prodigy, a natural. At the age of four, with no lessons at all, little Wally began tentatively playing on the piano keyboard the melodies he heard the much older George practicing on his violin. Once he began formal lessons, his improvement was rapid and dramatic.

A shy, solitary boy, the young Liberace spent his afternoons far from the baseball fields and fishing holes that his classmates frequented. He practiced the piano every day, for hours on end. In later life, he complained that his mother, who had immediately decided that her brilliant young son was destined to be a great classical musician, had pushed him too hard. "I never had a chance to be a kid," he lamented.

In 1926, when the budding genius was seven, he met the world-famous concert pianist and performer Ignacy Jan Paderewski, who performed as simply "Paderewski," a one-name tradition that Liberace would later emulate. The great man—an ardent patriot, he would twice head Poland's government—appeared in concert at the Pabst Theater in Milwaukee, where Sam Liberace sometimes played the French horn with the orchestra. When young Wally informed Paderewski that he knew how to play some of the pieces in the evening's program, the distinguished artist patted him on the head and said, "Some day this boy may take my place."

This story was endlessly repeated and wildly exaggerated by both Liberace and his mother. In one version the great Paderewski allegedly visited the humble Liberace bungalow to return a favor that Frances's mother had paid him long ago in Poland, and Wally flawlessly performed a Chopin piece for him. In this fanciful version of the story, Paderewski was overwhelmed with the boy's brilliance and pronounced him his protégé and musical heir. The Paderewski "legend" was not the only time that Liberace, like many popular artists, became quite accomplished at fashioning an image of himself that was at odds with reality. He often stretched the truth to make a better story: for many years, he lied about his age to seem younger, and he lied in print many times in trying to present himself as straight.

Wally was the kind of boy that schoolyard bullies would call a sissy. He played with his sister's dolls, creating elaborate imaginary characters. He enjoyed cooking and sewing. He learned to tap dance. But most of all, he played the piano, tickling those 88 keys to pluck the heartstrings of his doting mother and, eventually, the world. That he was a special boy with a special gift was obvious early in life. He longed for a world full of beautiful things, lovely sounds, fancy clothes, a world far removed from the poverty-stricken reality of his family home.

"Except for music, there wasn't much beauty in my childhood," he would later say. Music was his way of bringing light into his personal darkness. It was the ticket out of small-town Wisconsin that took him all the way to the stars.

He received help along the way, of course. Wally had an unfortunate speech impediment that caused him to talk too fast and in partial Italian and Polish accents. His sixth-grade teacher, Sylvia Becker, taught him how to use the "th" sound, which is not used in Polish or Italian. His

The future world-renowned pianist Wally Liberace (right) poses with his sister, Angie (center), and his older brother, George (left). All the Liberace children were given music lessons by their parents, but Wally's prodigious natural talent set him apart from his siblings.

lesson, aptly, included repeating the phrase "He was *the* Talk of *the* Town." Later on, Wally had several more years of speech therapy with Father Raphael Hamilton of Marquette University in Milwaukee.

But his most influential instructor, of course, was his piano teacher, Florence Bettray Kelly of the Wisconsin College of Music, a perceptive woman who saw in the young lad a real potential for greatness and arranged a scholarship to the school for him. His father had brought Wally to the college for an audition, seeking a teacher for his gifted son. Kelly was impressed with the boy's ability, although not with his attitude of superiority and disinterest in serious classical pieces. But young Walter Liberace could memorize in a single evening a difficult piece by Liszt or Chopin that would take another young musician a month of practice, and he and his equally strong-willed teacher often fought. Despite their disagreements, Liberace became Kelly's prize pupil, won many student competitions, and enjoyed the benefits of the longest scholarship tutelage (17 years) in the history of the college.

Liberace was one terrific musician, and his parents and Kelly were certain that someday he would dazzle audiences at Carnegie Hall, which he did, of course, but not in the way his elders had planned. While they were dreaming of a career in classical music for him, he was dreaming of something else. Something wilder.

CHAPTER TWO

WALTER BUSTER KEYS

*"Our Wally has already made his claim
With Paderewski, Gershwin, and others of fame."*
—From Liberace's high school yearbook, 1937,
West Milwaukee High

At the age of 10, Wally Liberace started having crushes on his male teachers. By the age of 14, he was playing the piano in a Milwaukee beer hall to contribute to his family's upkeep. At age 16, he was seduced by a man who came to hear him play in a bar—a member of the Green Bay Packers football team, according to the story he told a later lover, Scott Thorson. "I could hardly miss the guy," Liberace recalled. "Every time I looked out at the audience, there he was smiling at me. One night he asked to drive me home. That night I lost my virginity."

The football player became the boy's first adult male lover and introduced him to a network of others. In the 1930s, there were no openly gay bars or gathering places, but gay men met furtively and formed their

Liberace, photographed in his high school yearbook in 1937. His musical ability enabled him to win a scholarship to the Wisconsin College of Music.

own secret societies. Wally became a popular new addition to the circuit, and by age 18 he was leading a double life, socializing with his gay male friends every night, then returning to his mother's house to play the role of the dutiful son and budding classical genius.

Though by his mid-teens Liberace knew he was gay, and he was sexually active with other boys and with men, he felt pangs of guilt about it. He knew that his parents would not approve and that the tenets of his Catholic faith held such behavior to be sinful, and he felt ashamed. His schoolmates at West Milwaukee High School made crude jokes about "homos" and "fags" and "fruits," and he decided to keep his sexual orientation an absolute, enormous secret.

His family situation gave Liberace a certain foundation in deception. At about this time his father, Sam, fell in love with Zona Smrz, a concert musician he met through the orchestra, and he left Wally's mother for his new love. Frances forbade her children to reveal to anyone that their father had left home, so Liberace learned to conduct a life veiled in deceit. His nightly piano gigs in beery saloons and dance halls now became the family's principal source of income. Liberace would not see his father again for 12 years, and he found it difficult to forgive him.

Although not an athlete, Wally was popular in his high school. He never dated girls, but he played the piano at the school proms and was in constant demand to provide entertainment at parties. One year, for West Milwaukee High's annual Character Day, on which students came to school dressed as famous people, Wally dressed in full drag as movie star Greta Garbo. (In the 1930s, men could dress up as women for comic or theatrical purposes without necessarily raising speculation that they were gay.) He outperformed the girls in typing class and organized a cooking class for the boys, at the end of which they served meat loaf and corn muffins to their fathers. He was an outgoing, personable, friendly kid, always willing to help make a party a success. Wildly creative, he also made cloth corsages and sold them to the boys who had dates for the prom, eagerly signed up for every theatrical and musical production the school offered, dressed up in the best clothes he could afford, joined the German club, the Latin club, and the Hi-Lights Talent Show, and produced a girls' fashion show.

Wally made his musical debut at the age of 14 with a band of older teenagers, including West Milwaukee High students Del Krause, Joe Zingsheim, and Carl Lorenz. Their first date, in 1933, was at a speakeasy called Little Nick's in Milwaukee, where the patrons were more interested in consuming the local brew than in listening to the music. Sam Liberace, who was still living at home at the time, was furious when he learned that his son was playing music in a beer hall—but he could not deny that the family desperately needed the money young Wally was bringing in. The teenage piano whiz banged out such standards of the day as "Sweet Georgia Brown," "When the Saints Go Marching In," "Darktown Strutters Ball," and "Has Anybody Seen My Gal?" with ease and flair. It might not have been Mozart, but it was money.

One night when he was 16, Wally played for a silver wedding anniversary party at a place called Sam Pick's Club Madrid. The bridal party had presented the band with a bottle of gin, and Wally took his share of swigs. Inexperienced with alcohol, he got deliriously drunk and fell off the piano stool in the middle of a piece. From that humiliating experience, Liberace learned to drink alcohol only after the lights went down and the performance was over.

An infection presented a much more serious threat to his livelihood. When a hangnail became infected and led to blood poisoning and then gangrene in his hand, doctors recommended amputating his hand as the only way to save his arm and possibly his life. But Frances was determined to prevent her son from losing his potential career, and she applied a folk remedy she had learned from her Polish mother. She plunged the boy's arm into boiling water, smeared the infected hand with a poultice of milk and mustard, then wrapped the arm in wax paper. After five days and many applications of the old-fashioned poultice, pus began to escape, and Wally's hand and piano career were saved.

Just as with his hidden gay existence, Liberace also led a kind of double life in his musical career during his teens. He remained a star pupil of Florence Kelly's at the Wisconsin College of Music, supposedly preparing for a classical concert pianist's life, but he spent more and more time working low dives, bars, weddings, bar mitzvahs, anywhere he could pick up a few dollars playing the popular tunes of his day.

In 1939, he auditioned for conductor Frederick Stock of the Chicago Symphony and was invited to play with the symphony in its Milwaukee appearance. This great news was greeted with tears of joy by Wally's mother and teacher; it was to be his first step toward classical fame and a concert hall reputation. He did well in his performance of Liszt's

Liberace (far right, sitting at piano) poses with the orchestra for a mixer at West Milwaukee High School. By this time, he was an experienced performer who had been playing in bars and clubs for four years to help support his family.

Second Concerto in A Major and received his first newspaper review, "Young Pianist Proves Worth," by Richard S. Davis in the *Milwaukee Journal*. But the Chicago Symphony, aware that Liberace was also playing ragtime in smoky backroom saloons around town, asked him to change his name while performing in the beer halls. Hence, "Walter Buster Keys" was born at a dive called the Wunderbar in Wausau, Wisconsin. While "Liberace" stunned a highbrow symphony audience in his hand-me-down tuxedo borrowed from brother George, "Walter

Buster Keys" played for stag parties and got busted in a police raid on a strip show.

Liberace's dual talent for classical and popular music came together in a prophetic way at a small concert in La Crosse, Wisconsin, on an evening that would change his life. After playing a few pieces by Beethoven and Chopin, he turned to the audience—as was his habit—and asked if they had any special requests. Some joker in the balcony shouted out, "Play 'Three Little Fishies,'" which produced a ripple of laughter in the hall. It was a silly nonsense song made popular by Kay Kyser, which ended with a chorus of "They swam and they swam right over the dam." It was the number one hit in America, but a long way from Beethoven or even Irving Berlin.

Without hesitation, Liberace started playing "Three Little Fishies" and then played it in the style of the masters—"Three Little Fishies" as if it were written by Mozart, by Beethoven, by Liszt, and so forth. The audience roared with delight and gave him a standing ovation for his cleverness. Better yet, the Associated Press picked up the story as a novelty item and sent it out across its wires from coast to coast under the headline "3 Little Fishies Swim in Classical Sea." In one inspired moment of frivolity, Liberace had garnered more publicity than he had ever had in his life, and all because he had revamped the classical masters to entertain a contemporary audience.

The lesson was not lost on Wally. He started incorporating the joke into all his appearances. After finishing high school, he launched into an exhausting schedule of playing piano in theaters, lounges, and saloons at night, with occasional solos with visiting symphony orchestras. At 18, he was an accomplished professional musician, making more money at it than his father ever made playing the French horn, and "swimming" in a "sea" of gay friends in Wisconsin and the Chicago area.

"I realized," he later told Scott Thorson, "that a strong masculine body next to mine gave me a sense of security I'd never known before." But small-town life was not conducive to a life of freedom as a gay man, and Liberace tired of the charade of hiding his other self from his mother and family. He longed for a chance at the big time. He thought he would like to try New York City, where a bright young pianist might strike it rich—and might also meet quite a few handsome young men. In 1940, having just turned 21, he kissed his mother good-bye and set out for the Big Apple to make his fortune under the bright lights of Broadway—or die trying.

Walter Buster Keys was no more, and Wally was a kid's name. In honor of his hero, Paderewski, he started to perform as simply Liberace. In reverence to Chopin, as portrayed by Cornel Wilde in the movie *A Song to Remember,* he decided to place a candelabra on the piano while he performed, since the film depicted Chopin using one. The candelabra became his trademark.

Although certainly his real family name, Liberace was essentially a stage name, and the newly emerging young gentleman needed a nickname, something easier on the tongue. "Please," he told friends and lovers, "just call me Lee." And everyone did.

Lee Liberace hit New York City at the outset of World War II. (He had been excused from the draft because of a back condition.) His first stop was Times Square, where he met engaging young men and older fellows who took him in: he was invited to theaters, parties, and private clubs. Times Square during the Second World War was justly famous for its concentration of young gay men and hustlers. It was easily the "gayest" place in the United States, the place where it was always possible to find a casual boyfriend—especially if you were young and good-looking, as Lee was. Guys would simply strike up a conversation over a drink or have a quick romance in the back rows of a movie balcony. It was a safer and simpler world in the years before AIDS, and Times Square was the mecca for young gays on the loose. It provided Lee, for the first time in his life, with a place where he did not have to answer to anybody or hide his sexuality. His first days there were an exciting whirlwind of unlimited sexual freedom and the chance to make a name for himself in the musical world. He went hungry at first, surviving on ketchup and hot water "soup" at the Horn and Hardart cafeteria, but he knew the prize was out there for the grasping—the delicious prize of fame and musical recognition, together with love in the world of men.

CHAPTER THREE

"A BOFF CAFE ACT"

"The work of a cocktail pianist can be just as lonely as that of a concert pianist. For different reasons. In the lounge you soon learn that your audience didn't really come in to hear you. They came in for a whole catalogue of personal reasons involving getting a drink. A salesman wants to relax a prospect. A guy wants to make a girl. A fellow's been jilted and he wants to forget. He may be the only one listening to you."

—Liberace, in his autobiography

West Orange, New Jersey, was not exactly New York City, but it was close, and Lee had a job offer from an old friend and former Milwaukee bandleader, Jay Mills, to play piano at a restaurant-entertainment complex there called Pal's Cabin. It was a start. It was only a short trip into Manhattan, and Lee went there often to cruise Times Square, gaze at the lights of Broadway, and sneak into the second acts (after intermission) of operas, plays, and musicals for which he could not afford a ticket.

New York liberated his gay life also. For the first time, there was no authority figure looking over his

Liberace paints a keyboard and hands on a tie. In later years, his fascination with distinctive clothes would become more of an obsession, and he would spend up to $100,000 on clothing for each new show.

shoulder. He was free to go to parties and spend the night with men he encountered, without fear of being humiliated or found out. This blissful period of Lee's early twenties was one of the happiest times of his life, although he struggled financially and failed to make an immediate impression on the New York stage.

Pal's Cabin was not a bad gig. The customers were polite enough to listen to the music at least, and there Lee stumbled on a new idea that proved a hit. He spiced up classical favorites by abridging them to a much shorter length. He would do an entire Liszt concerto in six minutes, for example. People loved the act, and it attracted the attention of an agent, Mae Johnston, from the Music Corporation of America (MCA), who became Lee's first professional representative.

Using her connections and a bit of arm-twisting, Mae got Lee a job as intermission pianist at the exalted Persian Room at the Plaza Hotel in New York. He was not the star of the show, of course, but Liberace was definitely on his way. He was thrilled to do a warm-up act for such legendary stars as Hildegarde, Ella Fitzgerald, Imogene Coca, and Judy Holliday, and his $175-a-week salary was really good money in 1941 America.

The work itself was rather thankless. Customers used the intermission to eat and get drinks and talk loudly while waiting for the star performer to come on, and few people paid much attention to the young pianist. He longed for more and, meanwhile, studied closely the dashing theatrical style of Hildegarde, the frequent headliner. Born in Milwaukee, like Lee, she was a stunning blonde pianist and singer who moved her audiences to cheers with her flamboyant style, costumed chorus boys, trademark long-stemmed red roses, and theme song, "I'll Be Seeing You (In All the Old Familiar Places)." Liberace would eventually incorporate much of Hildegarde's grand manner, and even the song, into his own act.

He learned and grew. The Persian Room gig led to dates at other clubs like Spivy's Roof and Ruban Bleu. But the "big time" continued to elude the young pianist. His agent got him an offer to stand in for the bandleader Eddy Duchin while Duchin was away in the navy, but Lee refused. "I don't want to be another Eddy Duchin," he said. "I want to be myself." Disillusioned and far from rich, Lee decided to leave New York in 1942 and try his luck in Los Angeles.

A year earlier, while playing in Boston, he had met a shoe manufacturer from Los Angeles named Clarence Goodwin, who had told him, "If you ever get out to California, look me up." When Lee called, Goodwin and his wife were more than charming; they invited him to take a bedroom in their luxurious home, and Lee lived with them for over a year. Clarence Goodwin was so convinced of the young man's talent that he took over managing Lee's career, dismissed Mae Johnston and the MCA agents in New York, and bought Lee a magnificent Bluthner piano. With Goodwin as his agent, Lee found work in bars, lounges, and exclusive clubs in Hollywood and Long Beach, not to mention love and sex amid the throngs of young servicemen passing through wartime Los Angeles. The city was swarming with young men on their way to military service in the Pacific theater of World War II, and Lee had relationships with a number of sailors and soldiers as well as with the actors, dancers, singers, and stagehands of Hollywood, a town that has always welcomed gays, though insisting that they remain in the closet. His act developed with each passing month, evolving into a smoother, more professional routine, with added glitz and glamour. Meanwhile, his love life, like his candelabra, burned brightly. Los Angeles was a pleasant interlude for Lee, and Goodwin was a terrific patron and agent, but Liberace had not given up on New York and taking another shot at stardom.

Needing a new gimmick, he came up with the idea of performing live piano in synchronicity with recorded classical music by the great symphony orchestras and conductors. The act clicked, and when he auditioned again at the Persian Room at the Plaza, he was hired, at the staggering salary of $900 per week, to be the star performer following the engagement of—who else?—Hildegarde, putting Lee in the exalted category of his heroine.

The revamped act garnered Liberace his first "big" review, one of the few kind ones he ever received. It appeared in *Variety,* the "show business Bible," and was signed "Abel," short for Abel Green, who was the New York editor:

Liberace (right) greets composer Leonard Bernstein's dog in this 1947 photograph. The late 1940s brought Liberace a great deal of recognition, culminating in his 1949 performance at the White House.

Following Hildegarde into the Plaza's svelte room, Liberace brings a nice style to the big league nitery circuit with his legit and synchronized piano recital. It runs the gamut from synchronizing with the Boston Pops recording of Gershwin's "Rhapsody in Blue" (playing the Jesus Sanroma part) to a legit Chopin recital of the "Polonaise," Greig, "12th Street Rag," boogie-woogie, Beethoven and a novelty piano duet with a femme customer (who gets a token gift for her collaboration).

Liberace looks like a cross between Cary Grant and Robert Alda (who plays Gershwin in the Warner picture). He has an effective manner, attractive hands which he spotlights properly and, withal, rings the bell in a dramatically lighted, well-presented, showmanly routine. He should snowball into box office, which at the moment he's not, but he's definitely a boff cafe act.

The musicians' union pressured Lee to drop his recorded music, arguing that he was preventing working musicians from earning a living. He finally agreed, but the act of playing Gershwin's "Rhapsody in Blue" to a recorded accompaniment proved that he could handle the piece. He was invited to play it with Morton Gould and his orchestra on a national radio broadcast and eagerly accepted. Having only played a much shortened version in his act, he had to memorize the whole piece in a dizzying 40 hours of cram rehearsing. But he pulled it off brilliantly, and his first national radio concert brought his name into the homes of millions.

When the Persian Room engagement ended, Lee was swamped with other offers. He toured the finest and most expensive hotel nightclubs in the East and Midwest, plus parts of Canada. In Montreal, he met Leonard Bernstein, who was guest conducting the Montreal Symphony and invited Lee to appear with the orchestra. His star was rising rapidly. By the time he returned to Milwaukee's Pabst Theater, his engagement was completely sold out. The native son was beginning to make a name for himself all over the country.

The same *Milwaukee Journal* critic who had praised the youth's debut performance with the Chicago Symphony, Richard S. Davis, also reviewed the new act when it hit Milwaukee, but this time with some regret. Liberace, Davis wrote, has "turned his back on the concert platform and gone swaggering into nightclubs. . . . Friday night at Pabst, he gave a packed house the time of its life. He played the classics and played them well. He did amusing stunts with popular music. He pounded away at boogie-woogie. He even tried a bit of singing with his pale little voice."

In the front row sat Frances Liberace, beaming with pride. Her son Wally, the former Walter Buster Keys, was a star in his own right, filling

Liberace chats with jazz singer and tireless self-promoter Sophie Tucker at a party. He owed some of his biggest breaks in show business to the publicity techniques he learned from Tucker.

auditoriums all over the nation, making more money in a week than his father could earn in months of playing serious classical music. When he introduced his mother to the audience—which gave her a roaring ovation—Lee stumbled on to another of his famous trademarks. He was the flashy, schmaltzy, winking, funny piano player with the candelabra, the tuxedo, the irreverent style, *and* the doting mother in the front row.

But where to go next?

From the jazz singer Sophie Tucker, Liberace had learned an effective self-promotion technique. She used to mail postcards to talent agents, producers, and reviewers from every place she played, advertising herself and her availability. Lee started doing the same thing, sending out cheerful notes such as "booked solid here at the Statler Hilton in Boston." One of the cards paid off when he received a call in Montreal from Maxine Lewis at the Ramona Room of the Last Frontier Hotel in Las Vegas.

"Would you like to play Vegas?" she asked. "I'd love to," he replied. The salary was an unbelievable $1,500 a week. "But you'll get more," Maxine promised. "We paid Sophie Tucker $6,000."

Little did Lee know when he accepted that first Las Vegas engagement that he was about to find his Mecca, his real power base and spiritual hometown. Las Vegas and Liberace would cook!

CHAPTER FOUR

FROM THE LAST FRONTIER TO THE NEWEST

"For me, being known and successful beats obscurity all to hell."

—Liberace, on meeting Elvis Presley

The Ramona Room at the Last Frontier Hotel was a cowboy saloon, a far cry from the elegance of the Plaza in New York and the Montreal Symphony Orchestra. It had sawdust on the floors, wagon wheels for chandeliers, skimpily clad waitresses, and a rough, informal clientele. The place was more suited to the "Beer Barrel Polka" than to Beethoven, but Lee adjusted his act accordingly and proved a big hit. Instead of Beethoven and Brahms, he played boogie-woogie. He ditched his tuxedo and donned a playful cowboy hat and checkered western shirt. He encouraged the audience to whoop and yell "hey, hey." Instead of a standing ovation, he got whistles and cheers. Before long, the Last Frontier signed him to a 10-year contract calling for an annual engagement. It was the beginning of a life-long love affair between performer and city.

An elegant Liberace and his equally well-dressed mother, Frances, exhibit the familial affection that made her such a popular fixture at his concerts.

Las Vegas in 1945 was not the high-rise, neon-splashed metropolis of today but just a kind of gambling oasis in the desert that attracted some high rollers and organized-crime money. On his first day in the Ramona Room, Lee met Howard Hughes, the legendary industrialist and eccentric, but mistook him for a lighting technician and began giving him instructions until Maxine Lewis set him straight. Early in his Vegas career, Lee was also approached by the notorious gangster Bugsy Siegel, who tried to lure him from the Last Frontier to his new hotel, the Flamingo, but Siegel was gunned down by enemies before Lee could decide on the offer (which was $4,000 a week, double what he was getting at the Last Frontier).

Not only did Vegas pay Lee better than any other place had, but it also gave him the freedom to develop and enhance his act, experiment with ways to make himself more popular. There were no stuffy traditions, no protocols to follow. Liberace, "Mister Showmanship," the quintessential flash act, was really born in Vegas.

Aiding that transformation was the decision of Lee's older brother, George, upon his return from the navy in 1945, to become his kid brother's manager. George had come to realize that, despite his classical training in violin, he would never have the popular appeal Lee commanded, and rather than struggle as their father had with an ill-paying classical career, he went to work full-time promoting the Liberace name and legend. He made hotel arrangements, checked the microphones, rehearsed the backup bands, fielded press inquiries, and generally handled everything that Lee needed done while on tour. In turn, Liberace began introducing George as well as his mother at concerts, which now became a family affair.

The two brothers were destined to argue bitterly and, eventually, to split up, but the formative years of Liberace's career, when he first became a true superstar, were spent under his brother's management. They fought about Lee's extravagances—he was a spendthrift, while George was more conservative. Despite George's furious resistance, Lee insisted on bringing his own favorite piano with him on tour, at great expense. And they fought about Lee's homosexuality. George tried to discourage the gay men who idolized Lee and came to the stage door in hope of meeting him, and he complained loudly about Lee's open association with "fairies" and "fruits." George hired a press agent at $50 a week to issue news stories and photos that suggested Lee was dating or at least enjoying the company of eligible young women.

During World War II, every able-bodied young man who was not in the military was open to the suspicion of being homosexual, since the army began its policy of banning gays in 1940. Ironically, many homosexual men got into the service anyway, as the demand for manpower was so great during the war years. Only the most flamboyant or outspoken gays were turned away. Once in the military, gay men managed to enjoy each other's company despite official disapproval. Dressing up in drag and performing as females in theatrical shows was so common that nobody even thought of it as a gay thing, necessarily. Straight guys did it too. In New York City, young gay servicemen packed the balconies of the Metropolitan Opera—a traditional gay hangout—and the cheap movie theaters of 42nd Street in Times Square. The *New Yorker* magazine ran a cartoon depicting one sailor in New

Liberace and his brother George (right) install a statue of a young boy for a fountain. Lee's taste in home furnishings ran to the opulent and the homoerotic.

York City saying to another, "Lost, Sweetheart?" The war liberated thousands of young gay men from their families and small-town jobs, throwing them together in what amounted to a kind of golden age of youthful abandon.

Many of the actors, dancers, and singers Lee met in his touring days were gay, like himself. The combination of available servicemen and openly gay theater people led to a constant, but secretive, series of affairs and one-night encounters for Lee, who was "in the closet" but openly gay in the sight of anyone who knew him well. His younger brother, Rudy, who still lived at home with their mother, even complained to her that Lee tried to take sexual advantage of him when they shared a bed during his visits.

The later 1940s brought new recognition and fame to Liberace as he progressed from being a cafe act to a national name. He performed at the White House for President Harry Truman and future president General Dwight D. Eisenhower and cajoled both of them into joining in a chorus. The White House concert in 1949 was widely reported and gave Lee the added stature of a performer who has been recognized at the top level. "I wish my wife and daughter could have been here," President Truman told Lee. "They would have loved it."

Lee discovered a book called *The Magic of Believing,* by Claude Bristol, that became his personal credo of self-esteem and belief in one's own abilities. *The Magic of Believing* was a national best-seller that was based on a fundamental concept that believing leads to creating reality:

> How many times have you heard it said, "Just believe you can do it, and you can!" Whatever the task, if it is begun with the belief you can do it, it will be done perfectly. Often belief enables a person to do what others think is impossible. . . . As you stand before the mirror, keep telling yourself that you are going to be an outstanding success, and nothing in the world is going to stop you. . . . Don't forget that every idea presented to the subconscious mind is going to be produced in its exact counterpart in objective life.

Lee was so captivated by this can-do philosophy that he later authorized a Special Liberace Edition of the book.

To top off Lee's rise, he appeared in his first major motion picture, *South Sea Sinner,* opposite sultry Shelley Winters, in the role of a piano player in a waterfront saloon. The movie role was a plum that Lee desperately wanted. Already very successful as a musician, making $3,000 a week and at the top of his field, he aspired to be a great actor as well. He *believed* he could do it.

So did Universal International Pictures, which produced the low-budget B picture, a steamy epic in which he accompanied Winters in jazzy numbers such as "It Had To Be You" and "Loneliest Gal in Town." He managed to convince the producers to let him play an abbreviated piece from a Liszt concerto with a candelabra on the piano, despite the tropical island setting. The movie did poorly at the box office and generally received bad reviews, but Liberace's few moments were greeted with polite applause in hometown Milwaukee.

Although never destined to become a movie star, Lee had proven that his unshakable belief could be transformed into action. He had done it, he had "starred" in a movie. What could be next for the soaring young performer? He had just turned 30 and had begun losing his hair, which he quickly replaced with the first of what would be many toupees and elaborate hairpieces.

In 1949, he bought his first house—the first of many. The home was in Sherman Oaks, in the San Fernando Valley outside of Los Angeles, and Lee put in a piano-shaped swimming pool that became almost as famous as the performer himself. Thousands of gawking tourists drove past the house, hundreds of whom literally climbed his walls to get a peek at the pool. A few, uninvited, even jumped in.

Lee invited his mother to give up her life in Wisconsin and move in with him. Thus began Liberace's 30-year commitment to his mother, whom he took care of, housed, fed, and provided with all kinds of luxurious amenities. Liberace's fans viewed this mother-son relationship as a cherished bond, but Scott Thorson later revealed that Lee had a tortured, guilt-driven obligation to his mother, whom in fact he viewed as a burden.

With the dawning of the 1950s, a major breakthrough in Liberace's career resulted from his signing with the management firm of Dick

Gabbe, Sam Lutz, and Seymour Heller. Relations between Lee and his brother George were already strained, but George remained part of Lee's act and on the payroll long after Gabbe, Lutz, and Heller came aboard. Seymour Heller, in particular, made Liberace's career his personal crusade and remained Lee's manager to the end of the entertainer's life. It was Heller who urged Don Fedderson, a TV producer from a new Los Angeles station, KLAC, to catch Liberace's act. That one evening changed Lee's life forever.

It was 1950, and Lee was playing at the Hotel del Coronado in San Diego, a stately old Victorian mansion on the beach accessible then only by ferryboat. Because of rainy weather, a mere 17 customers showed up for the performance, but Lee gave them their money's worth, as always. In that tiny audience were Don Fedderson from KLAC and Jack Hellman from *Variety* magazine, who visited Lee in his dressing room afterward.

Television was in its infancy at the time, but its popularity was rising fast. It was the great equalizer between rich and poor. While the wealthy could afford to attend concerts, plays, and movies at will,

Liberace's "dream car" on display in Los Angeles in 1954. By this time, his television show's popularity had made him and his signature piano-plus-candelabra nationally known.

the poor could only stay at home, without visual entertainment—that is, until the arrival of TV. The first rooftop antennae appeared not in Beverly Hills, but in the small bungalows of the working class.

Don Fedderson saw in Lee's act terrific potential for this new medium. On that fateful rainy night in San Diego, he told Lee, "Television is not one huge audience. It's a huge number of small audiences. . . . While you are entertaining them, you are their guest. It's a very personal kind of thing, and it's that personal sort of entertainment you gave us this evening. If you can produce this kind of show on TV, you'll be holding lightning in a bottle."

Lee, as usual, was ready for anything new. Fedderson set him up with a local show on KLAC, in which he winked at the camera, smiled at the audience, and generated intimate entertainment and a huge following. That local show led to a network slot as a summer replacement for Dinah Shore, then to Liberace's own syndicated half-hour TV show, which by 1952 was reaching 45 million people weekly over 180 stations—more than carried "I Love Lucy."

The impact of that syndicated half-hour show is difficult to overstate. Liberace made millions of dollars a year in a time when earning that much money was almost unthinkable. He became as famous as anyone in the world as the Liberace craze swept the nation and then foreign countries as well. Most of his fans were mature women, mothers and grandmothers, many over 70 years old.

One old lady in Massachusetts had never seen TV before, and she believed the people on TV could see and hear her, just as she could see and hear them. Liberace was her favorite, and when he came on the air, she got dressed up in her fanciest clothes, makeup, jewelry, and hairdo to look her best for him. I should know. She was my grandmother, and I was the kid who helped her get dressed.

Television brought Lee more than money and fame. It brought him stature, the rare distinction of being a one-named performer whose name was a household word all over the world. With such fame at his command, what other possible honor could thrill him? It would have to be a command performance for the queen of England!

CHAPTER FIVE

COMMAND
PERFORMANCE

"I'm not a daytime performer. Daylight is bright and plain, matter of fact, and very real. The sun shows things as they are. Nighttime is different. The stars twinkle, the moon casts a mysterious white light, the shadows take on beautiful shapes, everything becomes more glamorous and that's the way I like it."

—Liberace, from his autobiography

Lee and George Liberace are served chicken by their mother during a family cookout. Despite the popular notion that the Liberace family was closely knit, relations between Lee and the others were often strained, in part because his mother and George disapproved of his gay lovers.

Wild success and riches beyond belief! Wally Liberace, liberated forever from poverty and the plainness of his upbringing in Wisconsin, had become just plain Liberace, Lee to his friends, who seemed to include every important star of his time, including some royalty. He stayed in Cannes, France, in the home of movie mogul Jack Warner and partied with Grace Kelly, Prince Rainier of Monaco, Peter Ustinov, Elsa Maxwell, Danny Kaye, Rita Hayworth, and the fabulously wealthy potentate Aly Khan. On an excursion on Khan's yacht, Liberace was inadvertently left floating alone in the Mediterranean Sea but was rescued after an hour. He was an official guest of the government of Cuba, then headed by General Fulgencio Batista, where he was treated like royalty. He even received a note from the great film director Alfred Hitchcock, who called himself Lee's "great admirer."

He played the Hollywood Bowl, an outdoor arena, in 1953, at the peak of the TV show's popularity, and set an attendance record never since broken. (After the concert, security officers removed 2,000 seats deemed hazardous, so even sold-out events in the future could not match Lee's numbers.) The orchestra appeared in black tuxedos, and Lee realized he would seem like just a speck to people in the high upper rows of the massive amphitheater, so he wore a white tuxedo and tails to set himself off. That began a new tradition of appearing onstage in unconventional, even outrageous, attire.

He used the white tails again in his triumphant first appearance at Carnegie Hall in New York on September 23, 1953, a major milestone for any serious performer. Playing at Carnegie Hall was the pinnacle of achievement for a pianist, and Liberace made the most of it. The sellout crowd responded with roaring standing ovations, even though the newspaper critics hated his act and published horrible notices. The *New York Times,* in the person of Howard Taubman, and the *Herald Tribune,* in the person of John Crosby, agreed that Lee's act was unworthy of the great traditions of Carnegie Hall, but the public ate it up. Wrote Crosby in the *Herald Tribune,* "If women vote for Liberace as a piano player—and I'm sure they do—it raises questions about their competence to vote for anything." Taubman, meanwhile, damned him with faint praise: "[His] is a type of piano-playing frequently heard in cocktail lounges and is very pleasant to go with cocktails." In response to the stinging reviews, Lee said, "I cried all the way to the bank," coining a phrase that is now part of standard American slang.

Carnegie Hall was followed by massive, hugely successful concerts in Madison Square Garden in New York and the Cow Palace in San Francisco. Never in history had a piano player drawn such crowds. Lee followed the Ringling Brothers Circus into Madison Square Garden and joked that he could still smell the elephants. He proved more popular even than the circus, traditionally one of the Garden's biggest draws.

As Lee's star rose around the world, he received many fan letters and gifts from his adoring public but also suffered many cruel and mean-spirited anti-gay jokes. His somewhat effeminate mannerisms offended straight male viewers of his TV show. As was typical for gay male performers in his time, Lee began dating girls in an effort to appear straight for the benefit of his loyal following, a masquerade of straightness that was, and still is, practiced in Hollywood because of a firm belief that the public will not support an openly gay performer. Liberace was terrified of losing his (mostly female) audience if the truth came out. Given the conservative political and social climate of the 1950s, his fear was probably justified. A 1954 fan magazine described his three "engagements," all of which had been broken off, but nobody associated with Lee ever noticed him having a serious relationship with a woman.

Nonetheless, in late 1953—to the great dismay of his female fans, who seemed to prefer the image of a bachelor who loved and took care of his mother—Lee announced that he was engaged to marry Joanne Rio, a former neighbor of his in North Hollywood. Lee and Joanne were often photographed on dates together, but the courtship was brief and ended when Joanne's father, Eddie Rio, confronted Lee with evidence of his homosexuality. Twenty years later, in his 1973 autobiography, Lee accused Joanne of selling rights to the story of their "romance" to a magazine, saying that her betrayal was the reason he had broken off the engagement. He also described their friendship as "intimate." She in turn sued him for libel, stating that they had never had sex or been "intimate," and she won an out-of-court payment in settlement.

Lee opened the brand-new, nine-story Riviera Hotel in Las Vegas in 1954 at a salary of $50,000 a week, a new record. The previous high had been $35,000 a week, paid to Judy Garland and Marlene Dietrich. Liberace was sizzling. His wardrobe fetish was now in full evidence—with $10,000 costumes leading to $100,000 in clothing expenses for every new mounting of a show—as was his lifelong obsession with hairpieces and hair-color jobs. As his outfits and mannerisms grew

Liberace dines with Joanne Rio shortly after their engagement was announced. In all likelihood, he had no intention of giving up his gay life when he became engaged to Rio, but false engagements could provide him (as they did many other closeted gay celebrities) with an invaluable means of diverting inquiry into his love life.

progressively more outrageous and flamboyant, Lee suffered ever-greater hostility and antagonism from homophobes, most of it in the form of innuendo and "fag" jokes that made their way around the country. Straight men, in particular, seemed sure that Liberace was gay, but, of course, he never admitted it. When he walked on to the Riviera stage in a tuxedo jacket studded with 1.3 *million* tiny sequins, however, the whole world knew this guy was a dandy.

Following the small part in *South Sea Sinner,* Lee finally landed a starring role in a major Hollywood movie in 1955. Called *Sincerely Yours,* it was a drama about a pianist (played by Lee) who goes deaf just before he is to appear in a major concert. This time, the reviews were favorable, but the movie flopped at the box office anyway. Lee's career as a film actor was over, except for a brief, funny cameo appearance in the comedy *The Loved One* in 1965, in which he played an unctuous casket salesman in a mortuary, and a guest appearance in the MGM musical *Where the Boys Meet the Girls.*

With his mother, brother, and an entourage of relatives and employees, Lee visited Rome in 1955 and was thrilled to be invited to a private audience with Pope Pius XII at his summer mansion, Castel Gandolfo. Lee was nominally a Catholic all his life, although he did not attend mass regularly and otherwise violated a number of church rules, including its proscription against sex outside straight marriage. But his mother was a devout Catholic, and Lee seemed to be sincerely honored to be received by the pope.

In 1956, it really happened. The queen of England invited Lee to perform in London, a command performance that would climax the most tumultuous, publicized, and bittersweet concert tour in Liberace's entire career. His first grand appearance in England was a success, to be sure. As always, he packed the theaters, and wildly adoring crowds of female fans followed him everywhere. But the English tour would become infamous for another reason—for a newspaper review that accused Lee of being gay, causing him to sue for libel.

An American magazine, *Confidential,* also printed an article accusing Lee of being gay. Under the lurid headline, "Why Liberace's Theme Song Should Be 'Mad About the Boy,'" *Confidential* published an article alleging that Lee had made unwanted sexual advances to a young male press secretary in Dallas. Lee threatened to sue the magazine and won a $40,000 out-of-court settlement. The story may have had some basis in fact, but Lee was able to prove that he was not in Dallas on the day that the seduction allegedly occurred. Even if the story was true, *Confidential* did not have all its facts in place, so the magazine backed off and paid up.

In England, there was no settlement, and the libel trial was followed by millions of newspaper readers and TV viewers. The whole brouhaha started with Lee's arrival at Waterloo Station, from the *Queen Mary* ocean liner, on September 25, 1956. An overflow crowd practically tore the train station apart; police said they had never seen such mobs except for appearances by royalty. Women clutched at Liberace's clothing and screamed, but meanwhile a group of men picketed with signs reading "Queer Go Home," "Yankee Fairy," and "We Hate Liberace."

The most acid insult of all, however, was the column written by William Connor, under the pen name Cassandra, in the *London Daily Mirror,* a paper with a circulation of 4.5 million. This piece, the basis of Lee's libel suit, seems rather mild in today's world of explicit sex in the media and outrageous tabloid newspapers like the *National Enquirer* and the *Star.* Even the gay insults are more suggestive than direct. Connor wrote:

> He is the summit of sex—the pinnacle of masculine, feminine, and neuter. Everything that he, she, and it can ever want.

Liberace kisses the ring of Archbishop Richard J. Cushing of Boston. Although the pianist was not a devout Roman Catholic, he had a strong Catholic identity and was thrilled to be granted an audience with Pope Pius XII in 1955.

I have spoken to sad but kindly men on this newspaper who have met every celebrity coming from America for the past 30 years. They say that this deadly, winking, sniggering, snuggling, chromium-plated, scent-impregnated, luminous, quivering, giggling, fruit-flavored, mincing, ice-covered heap of mother love has had the biggest reception and impact on London since Charlie Chaplin arrived at the same station, Waterloo, on Sept. 12, 1921.

This appalling man—and I use the word appalling in no other than its true sense of terrifying—has hit this country in a way that is as violent as Churchill receiving the cheers on V-E Day.

He reeks with emetic language that can only make grown men long for a quiet corner, an aspidistra, a handkerchief, and the old heave-ho. Without doubt, he is the biggest sentimental vomit of all time. Slobbering over his mother, winking at his brother, and counting the cash at every second, this superb piece of calculating candy-floss has an answer for every situation.

Nobody since Aimee Semple McPherson has purveyed a bigger, richer and more varied slag heap of lilac-covered hokum. Nobody anywhere made so much money out of high-speed piano play with the ghost of Chopin gibbering at every note.

There must be something wrong with us that our teenagers longing for sex and our middle-aged matrons fed up with sex alike should fall for such a sugary mountain of jingling claptrap wrapped up in such a preposterous clown.

The key terms in the attack are "masculine, feminine, and neuter," "fruit-flavored," "mincing," and "lilac-covered." Lee argued in court that these words and the entire tone of the article suggested he was homosexual, which he swore under oath he was not. He won the case and a $22,400 judgment, a ridiculously small amount of money but for Liberace a vindication of principle. "Certainly my manhood had been seriously attacked," he wrote in his autobiography, "and with it my freedom . . . freedom from harassment, freedom from embarrassment and freedom to work at my profession."

He was not exaggerating. In the United States in the 1950s, the political climate fostered by Senator Joseph McCarthy's famous anti-communist hearings and J. Edgar Hoover's Federal Bureau of Investigation was fiercely homophobic. Anyone even suspected of being gay could have his career destroyed overnight. The psychiatric profession regarded homosexuality as a mental illness. And Lee knew that his fans would be enormously disturbed to learn he was gay; most were women who had romantic fantasies about the entertainer they adored.

The *Daily Mirror's* lawyer charged that "Liberace has a bee in his bonnet about being called homosexual." But despite the large numbers of young men who gathered around Lee's pool in Sherman Oaks dressed only in bikinis, despite his growing audacity and risky sexual encounters, Lee won his case, in large part because the public in general considered the accusation of gayness as a libel, a terrible thing to say about anyone, and the defense was unable to prove that he was gay. (Under English law, the defendant in a libel suit is obligated to prove that what he or she wrote is true, whereas in the United States the plaintiff must prove that the defendant wrote or published something harmful despite knowing that it was inaccurate, a subtle but important difference.) All those guys around Liberace's pool were private guests, and no one came forward to admit to having sex with him. He also successfully sued a popular British singer, Jimmy Thompson, who performed a mocking song about him in which he chanted,

My fan mail is simply tremendous
It's growing so fast my head whirls
I get more and more
They propose by the score
And at least one or two are from girls.

And he managed to live down a British headline that read, "Is Liberace a Man?" His tactic was to ignore the insults whenever possible and strike back whenever necessary. Once, while being viciously heckled by a gay-baiting man in the audience, Lee simply gave him an upraised middle finger and asked, "How do you like the ring on *this* one?" The laughter from the crowd drowned out the ugly taunts.

Liberace, the world's most popular entertainer, had definitely and positively served official notice in public that he was not gay. But in his private life he was 100 percent gay. He bought a house in Palm Springs,

Liberace receives a police escort in Boston, Massachusetts. Despite allegations made by the *London Daily Mirror* that he was a homosexual, his popularity among female fans failed to decline.

California, in 1957 and proceeded to fill it with eligible young gay men, until his brother George complained, "Goddamn it, Lee, how can you keep saying in public and in courtrooms that you're not a homosexual and then you hang out in the Springs with a bunch of faggots? You're gonna get nailed some day."

Three decades later, after Lee died of AIDS in Palm Springs, and after the truth about his sexuality came out, the *London Daily Mirror* announced it would sue his estate to retrieve the $22,400 libel payment.

CHAPTER SIX

THE SHADOW
OF DEATH

"To live young, eat the proper foods, get the proper rest and the right type of exercise and, whatever you do, do everything in moderation. Drinking, smoking, sex . . . all in moderation. The joy of that is that you get to do everything longer, particularly sex."

—Liberace, in his autobiography

The late 1950s and early 1960s was a period of transition for Liberace in which his career, so electrifying at the start, slowed down and almost crashed, yet in the end was successfully revived. His mother was brutally attacked at the piano-pool house, his TV show canceled, and his brother George cast adrift. On the fateful day that President John F. Kennedy was assassinated, Liberace himself almost died, and he spent all his money from his hospital bed, buying lavish gifts for his friends and relatives because the doctors had given him a death sentence.

By 1957, Lee was spending most of his free time in his Palm Springs house, which was always full of

Liberace, surrounded by fans, is escorted from the court building after a hearing in his successful libel suit against the *London Daily Mirror*.

57

good-looking young men, most of whom spent their time lounging by his pool. George's complaints about the blatant homosexual activity at the home led to even more stress between the two, and Lee finally fired his brother and even belittled him in public, saying, "George is in the frozen pizza business." Their mother stepped in and publicly complained that she loved both her sons and could not bear to see them quarreling. Lee and George staged a reunion, but George never managed Lee's career again. Many years later, however, Lee called on his brother to direct operations at the Liberace Museum in Las Vegas.

The third Liberace brother, Rudy, also lived very much in the shadow of his famous sibling. He had a serious problem with alcohol, indulging in weekend binges during which he became belligerent and beat his wife and children. He was able to hold a job during the week but seemed to fall to pieces on the weekend. Everything about young Rudy's life was tragic, including the way it ended. He was found dead in a cheap Los Angeles motel room on April 30, 1957, at the age of 27. Lee was hysterical with grief at the funeral. In fact, Lee had not seemed particularly sympathetic to Rudy's problems while the younger man was alive. Furious with him for arriving drunk at one of his parties, Lee had kicked him out of his home and refused to provide support. But when Rudy died, Lee sobbed, "He was such a beautiful kid."

While Lee was on a concert tour in July 1957, his mother was attacked at the piano-pool Sherman Oaks home one night. She reported being mugged by two men wearing black hoods over their faces, who kicked her repeatedly and inflicted contusions, a broken rib, and bruises but never even tried to burglarize the house. The police speculated that Lee might have had enemies trying to get at him by hurting his mother, but the case was never solved. The ugly incident shocked Lee into selling the famous house and retreating into greater privacy in a new house off Sunset Strip in Hollywood and adding three additional homes to the one he already owned in Palm Springs.

After stockpiling so many smaller houses in Palm Springs, Lee eventually purchased the Cloisters Estate on Alejo Road, which would become his favorite and permanent home. It had been a 32-room hotel at one time but had fallen into disrepair. The asking price was $210,000,

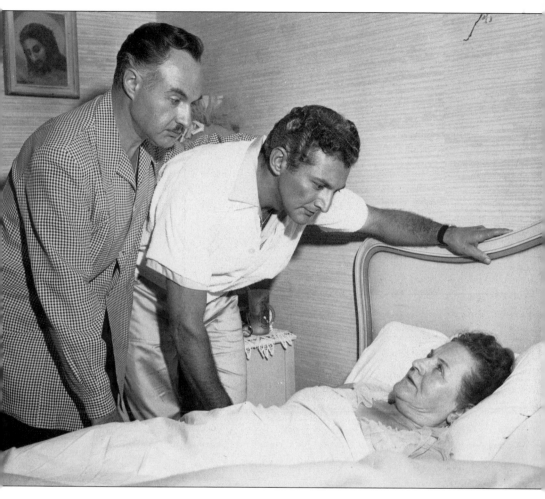

George and Lee Liberace visit their mother in the hospital after she was beaten by two men outside one of Lee's houses. Nothing was stolen during the attack, which the police suspected was aimed at Lee. The assailants were never apprehended.

but Lee paid only $185,000 for the Cloisters, according to his longtime publicist, Jamie James. "He considered it too cheap to pass up," James said. After spending another $136,000 to restore the place to its former grandeur, Lee created a truly grand mansion in his own kinky style. His toilet was a throne, with armrests and a high, red-velvet back. The shower curtain featured replicas of Michelangelo's *David*. There was a Gloria Vanderbilt suite, a Rudolph Valentino room, a Marie Antoinette suite, a room wallpapered in fake tiger skin, a pool-sized Jacuzzi, a personal chapel with stained-glass windows, a Persian tent room for fantasies of Arabian nights, an Olympic-sized pool, four courtyards, a U-shaped driveway, and a fountain in the shape of a naked boy embracing a swan.

Into this plush universe, Lee moved his mother for safekeeping. She had her own little cottage in the back. She continued to complain about the steady flow of young men through the Cloisters, boys and men she called "hillbillies" and "freeloaders." "But Mom," said Lee, "they amuse me."

Lee's career started faltering badly in 1957, however. The original Liberace TV show had gone off the air after Lee's managers decided he could make more money on the live performance circuit if he limited his exposure on free TV. Booked for four weeks in the Palace Theater in New York, he was forced to close the show after two. His lawyer, John Jacobs, caused a rift between Lee and his manager, Seymour Heller, which led to Heller's firing and further box-office flops. ABC television briefly introduced a new Liberace show, a daytime variety program in which Lee discarded the candelabra and fancy clothes and appeared in a conservative suit, but the ratings were disastrous and the show was canceled. Then came the absolute nightmare of his 1959 tour of Australia.

The February goodwill Down Under tour got off to a bad start. Arriving in the sweltering heat (Australia's summer being December through March), Lee discovered he was competing for press attention with the visiting Queen Mother of England, who was holding an afternoon reception in Sydney. Lee found an invitation to the royal party in his hotel room, embossed with the royal seal. Thrilled, he put on his best suit and attended the event, only to be denied a chance to meet the Queen Mother.

The press said he had sneaked in, that his invitation was a forgery. Lee claimed innocence. "Liberace Crashed Royal Party—They Wanted to Throw Him Out," read the headline in the *Melbourne Sun*.

The *Sydney Observer* called him a "pompadoured sissy." And his show, which opened at the Trocadero the following night, was greeted with an avalanche of hostile, scathing reviews—but, typically, drew a full house of cheering fans.

The cheers turned to boos after only one performance, however, when Lee was served with an injunction to stop playing songs from the musical *My Fair Lady* and he stormed off the stage in disgust. Although the musical was a big hit in the United States, it had not yet opened in Australia, and the copyright holder, Chappell and Company, threatened to have Lee arrested if he played even one more note from *My Fair Lady*.

The songs were an important part of his act, and Lee flew into a rage. On the second day of the tour, he stood onstage and orated. "Any laws that prevent my democratic right to perform the music of my country are in violation of the doctrines of my government and its people and must be interpreted as communistic," he told his audience while explaining that he would not perform. "Until I am once again permitted to perform any and all music of my country without any further restrictions, I am compelled by my American convictions and beliefs to refuse to give any further performances in Australia. I am truly sorry," he said and left the stage to loud murmurs and boos.

Lee's diatribe against communism was one of the very few times he made any pronouncement of his political views. He was parroting the prevailing anti-communist hysteria of the times, but it is not clear that he really knew what he was talking about. For one thing, the laws protecting music copyrights were capitalistic, not communistic. Lee appeared to have no interest in politics whatsoever, and for most of his life he refused to make political statements or publicly support candidates for office, for fear of alienating fans who might have different views.

After his announcement, a mob of enraged fans shouted insults and demanded refunds. Newspaper headlines screamed "Booing Crowds Held Back from Liberace" and "Liberace Walked Out—Thousands Booed." Lee received death threats. A judge fined him for copyright infringement and accused him of "acting like a petulant child." Crushed by the terrible publicity, which reached all the way back to the United States, Lee had to apologize and continue to do his shows despite dwindling audiences.

As 1960 dawned, Lee's career hit bottom. Without a TV contract, and especially without Seymour Heller's management, he seemed

Liberace shakes hands with Queen Mother Elizabeth of England four months after being denied the opportunity to meet her in Australia. The negative publicity surrounding his Australian tour reached all the way to the United States and further damaged his faltering career.

adrift. After being the world's most highly paid entertainer, he could not even land a guest appearance on TV talk shows, and he played concert dates in Oshkosh, Wisconsin, and Indianapolis, Indiana, rather than in New York or Hollywood.

Lee decided to return to his basics: his belief in himself; the philosophy espoused in Claude Bristol's book *The Magic of Believing;* his outrageous clothing and personal style; and his trusted manager, Heller, whom he rehired in an emotional reconciliation. The strategy worked. As the early 1960s unfolded, his popularity seemed to resurge, with Heller carefully booking him into high-gloss Las Vegas hotels and arranging just the occasional TV special to keep the public interested. By 1963, thanks to skillful management and his own "famous name," Lee was again on top of the world, pulling down record money at the new Riviera Hotel in Vegas, where he introduced a new young singer as his protégée. She had a large nose and a poor grasp of fashion, but the girl could sing like Fanny Brice or Ethel Merman, earlier sirens of Broadway. Her name was Barbra Streisand, and her performance with Lee's act caught the attention of producers Ray Stark and Jule Styne, who signed her to star in *Funny Girl* on Broadway.

Lee loved to tell the story of how he "discovered" the great Streisand, although in fact she had already had one small part on Broadway and had made two albums for Columbia Records before joining Lee's act in Las Vegas. He did much to promote her career, however, and they became close friends. And he always joked about what a lousy cook Streisand was, compared to himself. She baked a cake and asked Lee whether he liked it. "The frosting's a bit tough," he complained. "Oh, I ran out of sugar so I used flour instead," she replied.

On November 22, 1963, the day President John F. Kennedy was assassinated in Dallas, Lee was playing the Holiday Club in Pittsburgh. Earlier in the day, he had noticed that some of his costumes needed cleaning. Because of a snowstorm, the hotel cleaning person was not on duty, so Lee went to a hardware store and bought a can of cleaning fluid, using it liberally to wipe out the spots.

When the news of Kennedy's death flashed across the TV screen, Lee was devastated. Nominally a Catholic, he had supported America's first Catholic president enthusiastically. Certain that his scheduled performance would be canceled that evening, he collapsed on the bed and fell asleep.

When he woke up, it was to the news that the audience was waiting and he must perform—but he felt groggy, nauseated, and extremely ill. "The show must go on," said Lee, who tried to perform for the small and mournful audience but was soon overcome. He nearly vomited, finished only one piano piece, and staggered offstage, where he collapsed and was rushed to St. Francis Hospital.

The doctors quickly figured out that Lee's kidneys had quit working. He was the victim of uremic poisoning, caused by the carbon tetrachloride in the cleaning fluid he had inhaled during the afternoon. The physicians could do little to help him, and his condition continued to deteriorate until he was teetering on the edge of death.

After a day in which Lee got continually worse and his kidneys failed to respond to treatment, his personal physician, Dr. Frank Taylor, told him bluntly that he was not expected to live and should get his affairs in order. A Catholic priest came and delivered the last rites of the church. Lee's manager and accountant tallied up his available cash worth at around three-quarters of a million dollars, which he then proceeded to give away to his friends and family, ordering elaborate gifts from his deathbed.

He bought a house for his sister, Angelina. His mother received a mink coat and fabulous jewelry. The people who worked for him got sports cars, fur coats, diamonds, gold. He wanted to be generous with his friends before he died.

But he survived. Lee claimed he was visited in the night by a nun in a white habit who told him, "Pray to Saint Anthony. He works miracles." He prayed to Saint Anthony, he said, and miraculously recovered. But the nuns in charge at St. Francis Hospital said they had no members who wore white habits, and the doctors could find no logical explanation for his sudden turn for the better.

In any case, Lee's whole attitude toward life changed after this brush with death. He became less of a workaholic, more devoted to his houses, hobbies, and his passion for young men. He came so close to dying that he decided to really enjoy living.

He felt that he had been spared by God, saved from certain death. According to Scott Thorson, "He'd done things the church regarded as sins—sodomy, homosexual acts with multiple partners—but God had spared him anyway. From 1963 on, Lee, believing there was no sin too great for God's forgiveness, would stop at nothing in his pursuit of pleasures." Those pleasures included dining, shopping, all-night parties, and most particularly, most importantly—relationships with men much younger than the middle-aged pianist.

CHAPTER SEVEN

TWENTY-FIVE YEARS IN SHOW BIZ, FIFTY IN LIFE

"He takes his audience on a ride that is beset with familiar and pleasant landmarks. He trods no new musical paths. . . . He gives the impression of a handsome, graying man rambling along the keys in the living room. Kinda makes you want to hold hands with mother."

—*Variety* review, 1964

Liberace celebrates his 48th birthday outside the Hotel Sahara in Las Vegas. By this time, his career had completely rebounded, and he regularly received top billing in Las Vegas resorts.

In 1964, as Lee's career was rebounding from its disastrous fall, he found himself stuck in a rut. He was making good money, certainly, but he had not returned to the wildly successful level of his early days. Meanwhile, rock and roll had become a part of the American scene, and Elvis Presley was the king of popular music in America, a role Lee had enjoyed a decade earlier. The rock musicians were more outrageous than Lee had ever been, so he had to liven up his act and make his costumes more flamboyant than ever just to get noticed.

Elvis himself came to visit Lee in his Las Vegas dressing room, and the two swapped clothes and instruments for a publicity photo. Elvis played the piano in Lee's sequined sports coat, while Lee strummed the guitar in Elvis's striped jacket.

A young Texan named Jamie James became Lee's publicist in 1964 and remained with him to the end of his life. James was just out of college, wearing Levis and inexperienced, when he wandered into Lee's life, invited by a friend to a party at Lee's Hollywood mansion off Sunset Strip. Liberace took to him immediately, as did his black cook, Gladys Luckie, another Texas native and lifelong employee. James learned the publicity business from a master. Lee was adept at manipulating the press in interviews, even though reviewers usually gave him a bad time.

It was James who in 1965 masterminded the 25th anniversary of Lee's show business career, an extravaganza of free publicity. He gave lengthy interviews to *Time* magazine, the *New York Times,* the *Los Angeles Times,* and others, reflecting on his quarter-century in the entertainment field and the many changes that he had seen. But Liberace remained essentially the same. He still played the piano, had the candelabra and the glittering wardrobe and the undying loyalty of millions of (mostly elderly) fans. He was making $800,000 a year in 1965, not on a par with Elvis, but not bad.

For a brief time, he tried owning and operating a retail store in Los Angeles but lost money at the business and got out of it. The place was called Liberace Interiors and Objets d'Art and was stocked with antiques and statues, furniture and bric-a-brac from Lee's personal collection of items that he had bought all over Europe and America. He was an inveterate shopper and pack rat, unable to throw anything away, and kept his goods in warehouses when his homes got too full.

"My houses are full of a strange mixture of valuable antiques and junk, all of it chosen by me," Lee wrote. "I've arranged to have my homes left just as they are and maintained as museums. This will happen when I get too old or too tired to enjoy them. In the meantime, I'll continue to fill them with whatever beautiful things strike my fancy," he added.

Las Vegas continued to be a real gold mine for Lee, the one town where his popularity never faded. Seymour Heller stopped trying to book him into huge outdoor arenas, concentrating instead on maintaining headliner status and drawing smaller, but enthusiastic, crowds in Vegas. Because of his enduring appeal to elderly female customers, Liberace got top billing at the Hilton, the Riviera, and Caesar's Palace. His act grew progressively more flamboyant. He paraded with a brass band while wearing custom-made "hot pants," a popular, sexy kind of shorts. He made his entrance by jumping out of a 10-foot-tall cake. He

Liberace and Elvis Presley try each other's instruments and jackets. The popularity of rock and roll, which was noted for its energy and wildness, compelled Liberace to make his shows even more extravagant and lively.

sashayed onstage in a full-length ermine fur coat and peeled it off to reveal wings. He "flew" suspended from wires. And he was witty enough to make fun of his own extremes. "I'm no good," he would tell the audience, "but I've got guts!" One reason it was hard for critics to make fun of Lee was that he was always making fun of himself. He certainly was never pompous or stiff. Displaying his latest dazzling outfit to an audience, he would say, "Look me over, I didn't dress this way to go unnoticed." Or he would show his bulging rings to the audience, saying, "I hope you like them, you paid for them." And he often said, "This is so much fun, I'm ashamed to take the money. But I will."

After closing an engagement in Las Vegas, Lee enjoyed hosting all-male parties for his gay friends. He would rent a caravan of stretch limousines and treat his male friends to cocktails, dinner, shows, and all-night gambling, followed by a lavish breakfast at dawn. Usually, one fellow—Lee's favorite of the moment—would stay behind with him after the others had left. He lavished gifts of jewelry, money, cars, and clothing on these temporary boyfriends and had many one-night affairs and casual romances. It was not until later in life that Lee would get "serious" about one man, entering into a long-term relationship that would culminate in a "palimony" lawsuit.

In this respect, Lee was typical of many gay men of his generation. It was difficult at best to establish a long-term relationship with a lover in a country and time permeated with anti-gay prejudice pumped out by churches, psychiatrists, movies, the government, schools, politicians, and journalists. It was positively unsafe for a prominent public figure such as Lee to settle down with a male lover. The one-night stands and well-paid trade may have been part of a self-esteem problem rooted in Lee's shame at being gay.

In 1969, Lee returned to England for the first time since his infamous libel suit against Cassandra and found that a steady stream of reruns of his television show had actually increased his popularity. He taped a series of television specials in London that were shown in the United States that summer as a replacement for "The Red Skelton Show," and he made a number of guest appearances on other American television shows. The new "Liberace Show" turned out to be only a summer

Liberace climbs a ladder to put the finishing touches on his Christmas decorations. During the holidays, traffic jams abounded in his neighborhood as motorists stopped to look at the house.

series, but the publicity it generated kept Lee in the public eye and at the top of the nightclub circuit.

London had also changed since the arrival of the Beatles, a rock-and-roll group that was as popular as Jesus, according to the group's leader, John Lennon. "They didn't impress me as performers," Lee would later say about the Fab Four, "but I thought their music was wonderful.

Although Lennon and McCartney were not great musicians, they were terrific composers." Lee claimed that his own versions of the Beatles' songs were better than the group's originals.

As Lee turned 50 years old on May 16, 1969, he took stock of his life at the half-century mark. His following was completely loyal, his fame worldwide, and he was convinced he might live to be 100. He claimed to be taking a youth drug given to him by Marlene Dietrich. "Older people want to live longer, while the young ones are killing themselves with pot, and worse," he said.

His lifelong love of cooking brought Lee a new honor in 1970, when he became the best-selling author of a cookbook. *Liberace Cooks* offered recipes "from his seven dining rooms," where Lee himself was able to turn out dinners for his guests ranging from the simple to the gourmet. He served fine wines and did not like guests who took more than three cocktails.

One of Lee's favorite cooking stories involved the evening he baked a homemade lasagna for a dozen guests. While checking on the dish, he grabbed a container of what he thought was Parmesan cheese and liberally sprinkled it on the lasagna, only to find in horror that he had poisoned the dinner with Comet cleanser. Without batting an eyelash, Lee called a restaurant and ordered delivery of chicken dinners for 12, then raced back to the dining table and announced, "Have a little more wine, folks, dinner will be ready in a few minutes."

Lee saved his most lavish entertaining for Christmas, his favorite holiday and one that he celebrated with extravagance. Every year, he invited his entire staff and their wives and children, plus personal friends and members of his family, to one of his sumptuous houses, which he would have decorated with over $25,000 in ornaments and lights. He gave expensive gifts to everyone but hated it when people took his gifts for granted. One year, Seymour Heller hinted to Liberace that he might enjoy a Porsche automobile as a Christmas present. Lee gathered the clan around, gave Heller a gift-wrapped parking sign, "Porsches Only," then a miniature toy Porsche. While the crowd laughed, Lee turned around and gave his manager his real gift that year—a mink-lined leather coat. Nobody went away feeling cheated.

Lee was certainly generous, but his frenzied gift giving also tended to be rather self-serving. He gave only to people who worked for him or otherwise served his needs, and he demanded slavish loyalty in return. And he indulged himself in "showing off" by lavishing expensive presents on those well beneath his income level in a way that forced them to gush their appreciation.

Heller arranged a fantastic concert tour for Lee one Christmas season, one of the most lucrative offers Lee had ever received, but he turned it down. "I don't want to leave home at Christmas," he said, continuing his tradition of declining all bookings in December. "My orchids are in bloom in Palm Springs!"

CHAPTER EIGHT

FREE AT LAST

"My sexual feelings are the same as most people's. I'm against the practice of homosexuality because it offends convention and society. The only reason I never got married is because I come from a family of divorce. I'm so tired of people writing stories about me that are cancerous with innuendo."

—Liberace, 1973, in an interview,
"I Am Not a Homosexual, Says Liberace"

Liberace "flies" onstage at the Las Vegas Hilton Hotel. As his shows grew more excessive, he started to attract younger audiences who saw him as a campy cult figure.

Though his gay friends were horrified, Lee in 1973 was still protesting that he was straight, even though the famous 1969 Stonewall Rebellion in New York had launched the gay rights movement, and even though everyone close to him knew he was exclusively homosexual. Hollywood and music industry stars were still reluctant to come out, for fear of being ousted from the business and rejected by the fans. Even though they worked in the industry in large numbers, gays in Hollywood were forced to keep their sexual identity a secret. Anyone who dared to speak out or who got "caught" in a gay relationship could be ruined. Very few gay characters were ever presented on screen in the movies, but those few were portrayed in a negative light: gay men were always shown as weak, effeminate, and pathetic, while lesbians were hardly portrayed at all. Rock Hudson, for example, certainly never revealed his homosexuality until AIDS forced it into the open. But Lee went even further in hiding his sexuality. He figured that since his earlier libel trial in England had caused such a sensation, he would be exposed as "the world's biggest liar" if he now admitted to being gay. His whole reputation, he thought, depended on keeping up the biggest lie of his life.

Other than that, however, the 1970s brought Lee nothing but greater success and admiration. His pioneering outrageousness suddenly seemed tame in the face of revolutionary changes in fashion, music, politics, and morals. He pumped up his Las Vegas act, even drawing a smattering of younger people who viewed him as a kind of cult figure.

The Internal Revenue Service took notice of Lee's extravagance and pursued him for back taxes on a number of occasions. The government questioned his deductions for flashy clothing, limousines, and homes that were more like palaces. In Las Vegas, Lee had started out with a modest house, had bought three more, and had commissioned a replica of Michelangelo's Sistine Chapel to be painted on the bedroom ceiling. The courts ordered Lee to pay up, and he did, but he moved his legal residence to Nevada because it had no state income tax.

His passion for collecting things grew completely out of control. In the 1976 book *The Things I Love,* Lee showed off his dazzling array of expensive playthings, including a Baccarat crystal chandelier, a gold pipe organ, an onyx table, an 18th-century French bedroom set, a crystal table made for an Indian maharaja, a llama bedspread, an oil painting of Paderewski, a Chopin piano, a Tom Mix dinner service, a huge assortment of miniature pianos (some inlaid with diamonds), swimming pools, bars, jewelry, houses, a fleet of automobiles (with preference for Rolls-Royces and Cadillacs), and of course furs and a wardrobe almost too excessive to be believed. He had a blue shadow mink coat made from 100 pelts and a 25-foot cape of virgin white fox. Although he was bitterly criticized by animal rights advocates for his furs, Lee was fond

Liberace and pianist Vince Cardell conduct a press tour of the Liberace Museum. The museum was a financial success and also helped reconcile Lee with his brother George, who became the museum's manager.

of animals. He wrote lovingly about each of his many dogs, calling them his "babies."

In the same 1976 book, Lee wrote, "I suppose that as long as I remain a bachelor people are going to ask me why I have never married. . . . The unity of marriage is for me a sacred thing. I came very close to getting married two or three times, but some incident always occurred that gave me warning of what to expect. . . . I admit that I am intrigued by the tremendous urge to be loved. And I think, in order to satisfy that urge, I love tremendously in return. I love everybody."

It was a ridiculous exaggeration, of course. Lee did not "love everybody" and everybody did not love him. And the suggestion that he "came close to getting married" is a bold-faced lie. Perhaps he wanted to convince himself that he really would get married if the "right" girl came along. But it seems more likely that he fashioned the lie deliberately to keep his popularity and image intact. In any case, the ridicule and scorn that he endured in the early part of his career gave way to a renewed success and a salary of $300,000 a week at the new Hilton in Las Vegas.

His newest projects were the Liberace Foundation for the Performing and Creative Arts and the Liberace Museum. The foundation existed to provide financial support for young artists and musicians starting out in the business and was virtually the only charitable endeavor that Lee was known to contribute to. Unlike many stars, he never took on pet causes, donated to good works, or endorsed any political position. His Liberace Museum was meant to be a permanent showcase of his most lavish possessions, and he hired his brother George to manage it. In fact, the museum turned out to be almost too successful, becoming one of Las Vegas's major tourist attractions, and at one point Lee tried to find a way to disband his nonprofit corporation so he could keep the admissions proceeds.

Lee and Frances Liberace in 1973, seven years before her death. As she grew older, Frances became more demanding of her son.

George had also taken on the job of caring for their father, Sam Liberace, who turned 90 in 1975. Lee had never completely forgiven his father, and the two of them had never had a good relationship during Lee's adult life, but he did agree to visit the old man on his deathbed. "It's me, Walter," he said to Sam. The older man refused to believe him. "That's not my son," he said. Lee fled the meeting in tears, telling George, "Never try to persuade me to visit him again." Sam died on April 30, 1977.

Lee's mother was to die only a few years later, but she had insisted on remaining near her favorite son more than ever during the last years of her life. Bored and alone in the Palm Springs Cloisters complex while Lee spent more and more of his time in Las Vegas, she demanded to be moved closer to him. Lee bought her a condominium in Las Vegas and showered her with every material consideration, even her own slot machines, which he paid off when she hit a jackpot.

"Gladys (the housekeeper) would periodically come to me for additional playing money when Mom ran out of coins. She'd hit several jackpots but would never put her winnings back in the machines. Why should she? She had her own bank. ME!" Liberace wrote in 1986. Once, when Lee did not have enough money in the house to pay her off, his mother said, "That's all right, son. I'll take a check."

His mother could be a bit of a crank. Once, she insulted the cook by complaining, "My son has to eat meat loaf [one of Lee's favorite dishes] while the blacks in the kitchen are having New York steak!" Another time, she scared off the Japanese gardener by yelling, "Get the hell out of here, you goddamn Jap! What are you doing, planting rice?"

When his mother died on November 25, 1980, at age 89, Lee was 61 years old and felt free for the first time in his life. While he publicly adored her and pushed her forward for applause and adulation, he was, according to Scott Thorson in his tell-all memoir, *Behind the Candelabra: My Life with Liberace*, privately resentful of her bossiness and felt somewhat controlled by her. "Sometime late in the evening of the funeral, after everyone had gone," Thorson wrote, "Lee turned to me and made the only comment he would ever make about his mother's death. 'I'm finally *free*,' he said."

CHAPTER NINE

SCOTT THORSON, PART 1: HAPPY DAYS

*"Lee's had a string of boys like you. They come and go.
One day Lee will tell Seymour Heller to get rid of you."*
—Liberace's accountant, to Scott Thorson

By the time he met Scott Thorson in 1977, Lee had spent many years with a succession of young men, some of them still teenagers, who lived with him and received generous gifts from him, but all of these affairs were fairly short-lived. Liberace had a strong preference for the blond, blue-eyed, muscular type. After a few days, a week, a month, or more, Lee would become bored with the fellow (more often than not an empty-headed opportunist) and send him off with a final gift and a sigh. Some of the partings were more emotional, and a few were traumatic. After one young man walked out on Lee, he cried all the way from Palm Springs to Los Angeles in the back of his limousine.

But the temporary nature of these liaisons also saved Liberace from public embarrassment. As long as he

Liberace sparkles at an opening-night party in London. His wealth, fame, and generosity ensured him a steady supply of young lovers.

81

never got "serious" about a fellow, he could dismiss the kid as just another fling, a temporary dalliance that would never get into the newspapers or on the gossip circuit. There was safety in numbers, so to speak. Lee was never seen in public with the same young man more than once.

Scott Thorson changed all that. He not only moved in with Lee but became his intimate companion for a period of years. Lee once told his staff at a meeting, "The most important person in my life is Scott. His job is to make me smile, to keep me happy." Despite their age difference—Lee was nearly 60 and Scott only 18 when they met—they were inseparable. Scott even appeared in Lee's act, as the chauffeur who drove him onstage in a fancy car.

They met by chance, and young Scott had never even heard of Liberace on the day he met him. Born in Wisconsin, like Lee, Scott had an unstable childhood and by the age of 13 was a ward of the state. After knocking around various orphanages and foster homes, he was taken in by a couple with a ranch in northern California, where he was able to indulge his love of animals, a love that would be the first link to Liberace.

At 18, Scott was living in Los Angeles with a 40-year-old friend of Lee's named Bob Street, who took him to Las Vegas and introduced him to Lee in his dressing room after a performance. Never having seen Vegas before, Scott was dazzled by the bright lights and neon. Liberace seemed to like him instantly, and they started talking about Lee's dogs. When Scott said he worked with animals and knew of a medicine that might heal an eye infection in one of Lee's dogs, Lee immediately invited him to visit the following day.

The young man was overwhelmed from the moment he stepped into Lee's palatial home. Nothing in his experience had prepared him for such opulence. He was flattered, too, when Lee paid a lot of attention to him.

Two weeks later, Lee was on the phone to Scott in Los Angeles, offering him $300 a week and all expenses if he would come back to Las Vegas to be Lee's personal assistant and secretary. "But I can't type!" Scott protested. "Typing will not be necessary," Lee replied. It was

Donning a fur coat, Liberace prepares to leave Caesar's Palace in Las Vegas with a pair of well-dressed friends. His extravagant lifestyle often reached legendary proportions.

good money for the young man and a chance to live in great luxury. As Scott told it, he slept in the same bed with Liberace from the first night of his employment, they had sex for the first time on the second day, and for years thereafter they were lovers on a regular basis, although Scott found Lee unattractive because he was too old, fat (up to 250 pounds), and bald (he did not recognize Lee without his toupee). Scott enjoyed the lavish amenities of Lee's lifestyle, however.

Once Lee had rid himself of his previous young live-in boyfriend, he installed Scott as his reigning Adonis. He told him that he loved him—it was the first time that anyone had said "I love you" to Scott. Lee showered the youngster with jewelry, clothes, and cars. "All I had to do was admire something and it was mine," Scott later wrote.

"Our sexual relationship caused problems from the beginning. I'd completely underestimated Lee's sex drive. He may have been over the

"All I had to do was admire something and it was mine," Scott Thorson (right) said of Liberace's generous nature. But by the time this photograph was taken in 1981, he had become spoiled by Liberace's wealth; their love affair would end a short time later.

hill, but he wanted sexual encounters a couple of times a day," Scott claimed in his memoir. Lee used amyl nitrate, a stimulant known as poppers, to keep himself aroused; Scott refused the drug but admitted to using cocaine.

The first months of their union were like an extended honeymoon. Liberace was kind and protective toward Scott, who found himself thrust into a life he could never have imagined. Airplanes, hotel rooms, travel, restaurants, unlimited money to spend on expenses, fabulous clothing, and gushing expressions of love were all new things to the young man. If it was a bit of a nuisance to put up with Lee's sexual demands, it was worth the price to Scott.

They were together from morning to night. "I want to be everything to you," Lee said. "Father, brother, lover, and best friend. You make me young again."

Scott quickly understood that Liberace did not really feel close to anyone in his family, and that his friends were mostly employees. Lee talked of adopting Scott, making him his legal son. He even convinced Scott to undergo plastic surgery that would make him look more like a true Liberace offspring.

They fell into a routine built around Lee's show life. They went to bed around four in the morning, got up around noon or one in the afternoon. They went shopping together—Lee felt that a day without buying something was a day wasted. They were often seen in restaurants and were waited on by a full retinue of servants in Lee's many homes. When Lee incorporated Scott into his act, he went so far as to introduce Scott to the audience. Dressed in a white chauffeur uniform covered with rhinestones, white cap, and boots, Scott would drive Lee onstage in his $250,000 Rolls-Royce, open the door for him, and salute crisply. "I'd like you all to meet my friend and companion, Scott Thorson," Lee told the audience. "As far as I was concerned, Lee might as well have announced that we were lovers," Scott commented in his book, but "the fans never drew the obvious conclusion."

By the time he was living with Scott, Liberace had started poking fun at himself and making jokes onstage that came perilously close to admitting he was gay. "This is my sport coat," he said of a wildly glittering cape, "but I won't say which sport!" After decades of accusations and denials, Lee seemed to enjoy teasing the audience with suggestions of gayness without ever confessing anything. Sometimes he asked a woman in the audience if he could dance with her husband. When the husband (invariably) declined, Lee winked and said, "Maybe later," provoking raucous laughter. In the 1980s, when he was over 60, Lee finally achieved a lighter, more open attitude toward homosexuality. So did American society as a whole, as the issue became less controversial. Yet Lee never came out.

Their first Christmas together, Lee entrusted Scott with the important job of decorating his Las Vegas house for the holiday. He handed Scott $25,000 to spend on new ornaments to add to the thousands already in storage from previous years. Scott produced an extravaganza, including 18 Christmas trees, 350 poinsettias, decorations, candles, lights, and groaning banquet tables. Lee personally bought presents for all his "people," wrapped them himself, and laid them out under the trees in time for his traditional Christmas Eve dinner and party.

Scott's gifts from Lee that first Christmas included two diamond rings, two mink coats, a sapphire cross, a gold watch inlaid with diamonds, a coyote leather jacket, three pedigree dogs, and a mountain of new clothes. Scott was speechless. So were the members of Lee's staff, who privately noted that no previous boyfriend had ever made off with such a generous haul of gifts from Liberace.

It was only the beginning. Lee continued to lavish gifts on Scott year-round. One time, he gave him two cars in a single week, a Chevrolet Camaro and a Rolls-Royce. He even gave Scott a house in Las Vegas, to teach him the value of real estate investment, which was certainly one of Lee's primary passions. While living with Scott, Lee added to his Las Vegas and Palm Springs homes a beachfront condominium in Malibu, an office building with a penthouse apartment in Beverly Hills, a house in Lake Tahoe, and four extra condominiums in Las Vegas that he wanted just for the joy of redecorating them.

"Scott's house" was only a tiny six-room bungalow, but the lovers had a wonderful time there, with Lee reversing roles and pretending to be Scott's "wife," cleaning, dusting, and cooking dinner.

But the happy days of unlimited luxury had their dark side, too. Liberace was 40 years older than Scott, and a 60-year-old's idea of a good time is often not the same as a 20-year-old's. After he was finished performing, Lee wanted to stay home in privacy and rest. Scott craved more socializing, the company of people his own age. He got bored. He also had increasing difficulty accommodating Lee's sexual demands. After a tour ended, Lee would often get drunk on the plane home and make amorous advances toward Scott in full view of the flight attendants. "I'm not ashamed of being gay, but I hated being groped in public," Scott complained.

Age had taken its toll on Lee's appearance. The hairpieces and flashy costumes could not hide the wrinkles in his face, so he decided on a complete face-lift and engaged a prominent Beverly Hills surgeon. Then, he decided to have the same doctor alter Scott's appearance with a nose job, silicone implants, and a chin cleft to make Scott look more like his real son. According to Thorson, the doctor also prescribed a "California diet" for Scott, an amphetamine- and cocaine-laced oral medicine that killed Scott's appetite. Lee emerged from his surgery looking quite a bit younger, and Scott emerged looking quite a lot more like Lee.

In 1980, Lee drew up formal adoption papers that would have made Scott his legal son. But he never signed them. He became concerned that Scott was turning into a cocaine addict. Sex between the two of them became less frequent. Then, Lee started openly flirting with other boys. Scott claimed to be put off by Lee's intense passion for pornographic videos. The two began to argue and fight bitterly, each accusing the other of being unfaithful.

By 1981, something else had changed too. Scott was not 18 anymore, but 22. He was no longer an innocent lad dazzled by Liberace and all his glory, but (by his own admission) a spoiled, arrogant drug addict. Their love affair fizzling, their relationship on edge, Lee and Scott instinctively knew the end was near.

CHAPTER TEN

SCOTT THORSON, PART 2: SEPARATION AND REGRET

"Some people say that [sex] saps your creative energy, but I don't believe that. I think it's a very healthy thing. A healthy sex life keeps you young and vital. And it should be frequent."

—Liberace, quoted in the book *The First Time*

Early in 1982, Liberace met Cary James, an 18-year-old dancer in the Young Americans troupe, which performed with him in Las Vegas. Cary was young, good looking, and good natured, and Lee took to him. While Scott Thorson was away from home attending the funeral of his foster mother, Cary James spent the night with Lee. When Scott found out about it later, he was furious.

The betrayal was not unexpected, however. Though their relationship had been monogamous, Lee and Scott had been cooling toward each other, with Scott admitting to heavy cocaine abuse and Lee

Liberace after his performance at the Academy Awards ceremony on March 29, 1982, four days after he had Thorson evicted from his Beverly Hills apartment.

openly flirting with teenage boys as if Scott were not present. Scott also complained about Lee's preoccupation with pornography and suggestions of "kinky" sex, particularly the idea of three-way sex.

Their alienation grew until Scott moved out of the Palm Springs house and took refuge in Lee's penthouse apartment on Beverly Boulevard in Los Angeles. At the same time, Lee was entertaining two

Thorson (right) and his lawyer file a $113 million lawsuit against Liberace, claiming that Liberace had promised Thorson money and half of his real estate in exchange for companionship and sex.

French teenage boys as houseguests in Palm Springs. Upon hearing of the French visitors, Scott flew into a rage, destroying furniture in the apartment and phoning Lee to argue and complain bitterly.

The end came on March 25, 1982, when Lee's manager, Seymour Heller, and several armed security guards physically ousted Scott from the Beverly Hills apartment, evicting him along with three trash bags filled with his belongings. Later that day, Lee moved back into the same apartment after presenting the award for the best soundtrack at the Academy Awards.

Scott could not believe that he was literally on the street, dropped by Lee without a good-bye after five years of intimate life together. Nor did he have any alternative way of making a living. Lee, through his lawyers, gave him $75,000 as a settlement, but Scott maintained that he signed the settlement papers only because he was destitute and needed to get his clothing and property returned from Lee's houses.

On October 14, 1982, Scott filed a lawsuit seeking $113 million in damages from Liberace, alleging that Lee had promised him a lifetime income, half of his real estate, and a monthly salary in exchange for companionship and sex.

The *National Enquirer* broke the story: "Liberace Bombshell—Boyfriend Tells All—World Exclusive." The world press spread the story, and for the second time in his life, Lee was an international sensation because of a gay scandal.

Once again, he denied being gay. Lee retaliated in the *Enquirer's* rival tabloid, the *Globe,* under a headline that read, "Gays Out to Assassinate Me, Says Liberace." Lee's official response to Scott's suit was that Scott was a disgruntled employee with a drug problem, never a lover or a friend.

The suit dragged on for years through court hearings and depositions, charges and countercharges, but it never came to a full public trial and Lee never testified in person. On March 1, 1984, Nevada Superior Court judge Ricardo Torres found in favor of Lee over Scott on the grounds that Scott's contract "for sex" amounted to prostitution. By 1986, the Thorson lawyers had settled with Lee's lawyers, and Scott received a $95,000 payment to drop the suit.

Despite their bitter public separation and lawsuit, Lee called Scott several times that year to ask if his health was all right. Scott later interpreted these calls as warning signs that Lee had AIDS and was worried that Scott might be infected. But Lee never indicated to Scott or anyone else that he was seriously ill.

Liberace "plays" a piano made of ice after a performance at New York's Radio City Music Hall in 1984. Despite being engaged in a legal dispute with Thorson at the time, he was concerned about Thorson's health and later gave him a ring that had belonged to his mother.

Around Christmas that same year, Lee called Scott once more and asked him to visit him in Palm Springs. When he got there, Scott found Lee looking much slimmer, older, and ill. Lee gave Scott a gift of his mother's ring, saying, "You made me the happiest. Merry Christmas."

93

CHAPTER ELEVEN

BOUND FOR GLORY

*"I remember being very poor once and making a promise
to myself, if I could do anything about it, with God's help,
I'd never be poor again."*

—Liberace, in an early interview with Edward R. Murrow

Although the Thorson affair clearly and definitely indicated that Lee was gay, despite his denials, the public seemed unconcerned. Lee's popularity soared in the 1980s as never before. When even the steaming scandal of Scott Thorson did not harm Lee's career, he became ever more bold and outrageous in his act, often making sexual jokes—both gay and straight—and implying that he had a great sexual appetite. The public did not seem to care whether Lee was gay or straight; they simply loved his shtick.

Taking his act to Radio City Music Hall in New York City had long been one of Lee's cherished goals, one he had never realized in his long career. His manager, Seymour Heller, had not liked the idea. Lee's act was seen as "too Las Vegas," not sophisticated enough for New York, and Heller was convinced

Liberace displays his characteristically flamboyant and expensive jewelry. "To shake his hand is to flirt with laceration," wrote one interviewer.

that the New York critics would destroy Liberace if he dared play the concert stage in that town.

But Radio City Music Hall courted Lee from 1980 to 1983, and finally in 1984, during its annual "Glory of Easter" pageant, the legendary theater presented Liberace for 14 sold-out performances, breaking all its own attendance records. "You can have the Resurrection or you can have Liberace," Lee had proclaimed, "but you can't have them both."

Lee wasted no time in promoting the Radio City appearances. Against all odds, he appeared on the hip, cynical "Late Night with David Letterman" show on NBC, where he was such a hit that he was invited back several times. Once, he appeared on "Letterman" with rock idol Bob Dylan, and the two exchanged compliments and autographs. He went on "Saturday Night Live," even though the show subjected him to comic humiliation. He did Phil Donahue's show, gave cooking classes at Macy's department store, and participated in a glitzy promotion for Baldwin pianos. Real-estate tycoon Donald Trump invited Lee to take an apartment at the new Trump Tower as his guest, and there he entertained gossip columnist Liz Smith and soap opera star Linda Dano, one of his favorite actresses.

Mr. Showmanship poses in an extra-full-length fur coat with a bevy of showgirls and two dogs. Although he loved animals and had a number of cherished pets, he felt no qualms about wearing furs and owned dozens of them.

After 40 years in show business, Lee had earned the tribute of making his entrance on the Radio City stage while the band played the song "There's No Business Like Show Business." He wore 10 costumes worth $1 million, played five pianos, rode in three cars, danced with the famous Rockettes, and gave a smooth performance that even the conservative *New York Times* admitted was a "style that is not classical, jazz or pop but an ornamental genre unto itself . . . a one-of-a-kind musical monument."

Altogether, he sold 70,000 tickets for the two-week Easter engagement, and the audience was not restricted to old ladies. Young people and folks of all musical tastes came to see the living legend perform Chopin and Mozart "with the dull parts left out," movie theme songs, Gershwin requests. As usual, he had a "chauffeur and friend" onstage and showed off his huge rings to the audience, still saying, "Do you like them? You ought to—you paid for them." His new boyfriend, Cary James, was with him at all times.

Radio City decided that it simply had to have Liberace back, and so during Easter season in 1985, Lee took to the giant stage again, this time for 21 sold-out performances that were hyped by an avalanche of free media publicity. Every important TV talk show invited Lee on. He invented a new routine and made a grand entrance by jumping out of a huge egg while wearing pink feathers and a cape that weighed a hundred pounds. "I was the first to create shock waves," Lee told the press. He compared himself to Michael Jackson, Prince, and Boy George, younger performers who understood the value of glitz.

The return engagement merited a front-page feature in the *New York Times*. Reporter William E. Geist wrote, "To shake his hand is to flirt with laceration. Let's see, left to right we have the enormous topaz and gold ring, the grand piano of diamonds and gold with the top that opens, the simple hunk of amethyst ring, the diamond candelabra ring, the gold record-player ring with moving turntable, and a large gold structure of a ring that looks as if it were designed by Buckminster Fuller." When asked how he could play the piano with all those huge rings on his fingers, Lee always replied, "Very well, thank you."

Back in Milwaukee, Lee's hometown, the Veterans Administration announced it would restore the old Ward Theater (built in 1882) and rename it the Liberace Playhouse in Lee's honor. Lee was honored indeed and attended a gala launch of the public fund-raising drive, saying, "A lot of people have theaters named after them when they're dead. I'm glad I'm still alive to see this."

The fund-raising campaign fell short of its $1.6 million goal, however, and when the committee wrote to Liberace asking for a donation, he abruptly withdrew from the project and denied them permission to use his name on the building. Although generous almost to a fault with his friends and staff, Lee was never known to donate to "good causes."

As he grew older, Lee had more and more plastic surgery and used more makeup and hairpieces to try to retain a youthful appearance, but all these devices only made him look unreal. The death of his brother George on March 9, 1985, sent him into a prolonged depression. George had spent most of his later years being the official host at the Liberace Museum. He was buried alongside his mother at Forest Lawn in Glendale, California, and Lee seemed to understand that his own time was limited.

Liberace's popularity continued to grow, however. In 1985, he earned $3.5 million in a mere 14 weeks. His Las Vegas salary was up to $400,000 a week, and he routinely turned down $500,000 offers when he was not in the mood to perform. "I've become a hot ticket," he told the *Washington Post.* "The minute it gets out that you're not all that available, your price keeps going up."

The actress Shirley MacLaine helped Lee write his 1986 book, *The Wonderful Private World of Liberace,* a compendium of all his fabulous possessions. President Ronald Reagan invited him to the White House, and Lee brought along his housekeeper, Dorothy MacMahain, as his escort, after buying her a new gown and caps for her teeth. President Reagan's son, Ron junior, interviewed Lee on TV's "Good Morning, America."

Radio City asked Lee back for one more engagement in October and November of 1986. Nobody knew it at the time, but these were to be Liberace's final public appearances. At 67 years of age, he seemed

Liberace talks with fans outside the Ward Theater in Milwaukee, which the
Veterans Administration wanted to rebuild and rename the Liberace Playhouse.
Although he was initially flattered by the plans for the theater, he later withdrew
his support when the Veterans Administration asked him to contribute funds.

Boxer Muhammad Ali (left), Liberace, and wrestler Hulk Hogan (right) compare rings (and lack thereof). Liberace's popularity seemed to know no bounds in the mid-1980s, a time when his health was rapidly failing.

tired, thinner, lacking the same energy level. Even *Variety,* the show business paper, noticed. "The thrill is gone," the paper reported. "All the shticks which once were fresh, no longer have much excitement." Many people whispered behind his back that Lee did not look well, but he maintained that his health was fine, that he was losing weight only because of a watermelon diet.

He opened the music hall show by flying onstage on a wire, something he had started doing years before in Las Vegas. He was the

Peter Pan of the concert circuit, and the audience ate it up. Cary James was always in the wings, waiting to get him safely to his dressing room and out of the public eye. As always, he ended every show with the song "I'll Be Seeing You."

When the Radio City gig was over on November 3, 1986, Lee had played an amazing 56 performances for a total of more than 300,000 people. No other artist has attracted that number of people to the music hall, and perhaps no one ever will.

At the huge cast party afterwards, Lee seemed exhausted. He went home to the Cloisters in Palm Springs with Cary James and a secret in his heart. He had AIDS, but he did not want anyone to know.

The annual Christmas party was a subdued affair in 1986. Everybody noticed that Lee seemed frail and worn-out, but nobody knew why. The party was over by 10:30 P.M., and Lee's life was over a month and a half later.

CHAPTER TWELVE

I'LL BE SEEING YOU

"The most valuable and important thing in life is your health, and if you have that, you're a rich person."
—Liberace, in his final interview, December 1986

On January 22, 1987, Liberace signed his last will and testament with his backyard Palm Springs neighbors, Ken Fosler and Vince Fronza, as witnesses. He left his entire estate to the Liberace Foundation for the Performing and Creative Arts, a bequest that would later be challenged in court by his sister, Angie.

One day after signing the will, Lee entered the Eisenhower Medical Center in Palm Springs. On January 24, the *Las Vegas Sun* started a worldwide deathwatch when it printed the headline "Liberace Victim of Deadly AIDS." But Seymour Heller, Lee's spokesman, heatedly denied the rumor. Lee had simply lost weight on his new diet, Heller declared.

The world press descended on Palm Springs. The *National Enquirer* alone sent eight reporters. After Lee returned to the Cloisters from the hospital, large crowds began to gather outside the gates of the house,

Much to the dismay of his friends and family, Liberace's death proved to be as big a publicity event as anything in his life. The media circus surrounding his death was fueled in no small part by the national hysteria over AIDS, which at that time was a new disease to the general public.

waiting for word. Some were devoted fans, others just reacting to the media circus. Police kept pushing the crowds back, and some reporters and photographers were arrested for trespassing. Inside the house, Lee was bedridden and carefully prevented from watching any news shows on TV, all of which were filled with stories about his impending death.

His official news release to the public said Lee was sick with heart disease and emphysema, related to his lifelong cigarette-smoking habit. Denial of the AIDS diagnosis continued even after Lee had died.

"Is he dead yet?" people asked each other as the reporters camped in front of the house. A group of students from San Diego State

After his death, Liberace's many possessions were auctioned off to benefit the Liberace Foundation for the Performing and Creative Arts.

University drove to Palm Springs to set up a candlelight vigil. One of their friends at school had scoffed, "He's a fag. Why drive two hours to see a fag die?" The student driver replied, "Liberace is the best. He's got style. Elton John tried to copy him, but he was the original."

Elton John was one of the stars who sent flowers to Lee's sickbed, along with Tony Orlando and Tom Jones. As often happens with victims of AIDS, Lee gradually lost the ability to speak and could only nod yes or no in response to questions. Then he seemed to lose his eyesight, staring into space without recognition.

On February 4, 1987, the people closest to Lee gathered around him. Cary James was there; Seymour Heller; Lee's sister, Angie; his longtime cook, Gladys Luckie; George Liberace's widow, Dora; and his friendly Palm Springs neighbors, Ken and Vince.

The end came at 11:02 that morning. At 3:00 P.M., the news reporters were given a brief statement, and Lee's body was whisked away in an unmarked car, bound for Forest Lawn Cemetery, where his mother and George were already buried. Lee's staff asserted that he had died of heart failure, continuing to deny that he had AIDS. Workers at Forest Lawn attempted to bury him quickly, but the Riverside County coroner, Raymond Carillo, intervened and ordered Lee's body brought back for tests. "Somebody tried to pull a fast one on us," Carillo said angrily.

The tests proved beyond a doubt that AIDS was the cause of death, and Carillo announced it at a press conference at the same moment that celebrities and friends were gathering for Lee's Catholic funeral. Debbie Reynolds downplayed the AIDS scandal, saying, "Liberace was a wonderful man and should be remembered as a loving, dear person and not for any other reason."

Shirley MacLaine described Lee as "the nicest person in show business." Red Skelton called him the "P. T. Barnum of the symphony halls." Phyllis Diller said he was "the greatest positive thinker I've ever known." And Mickey Rooney added, "I loved him, as did the world."

Later, it was revealed that the only person other than his doctor who knew Lee had AIDS was his young boyfriend, Cary James. Even Seymour Heller had been kept in the dark.

The Liberace Museum in Las Vegas attracts visitors from all over the world, testifying to Liberace's enduring popularity as both a performer and a personality.

As in life, so in death, Lee was big news. He was on every television newscast and on page one in every newspaper. The *New York Times* obituary on February 5, 1987, fairly gushed:

> With his megawatt smile, his furry, feathery costumes, rhinestones as big as the Ritz, piano-shaped rings and a unique blend of Beethoven and the "Beer Barrel Polka," Liberace charmed millions with a flashiness that was almost too much to be believed.

The Cloisters in Palm Springs was opened to the public for the first time on April 8, 1990, and many of Lee's most prized belongings were auctioned off to the highest bidders. The auction benefited the Liberace Foundation for the Performing and Creative Arts.

Once again, curious onlookers swarmed over the grounds. For sale at whatever price they could bring were five pianos, two automobiles, furs, French and English furniture, Lee's miniature-car collection, a black diamond mink bedspread, a stuffed, naked male doll, and a statue of a boy embracing a swan.

FURTHER READING

Liberace, with Carroll Carroll. *Liberace: An Autobiography*. New York: Putnam, 1973.

———. *The Things I Love*. Edited by Tony Palmer. New York: Grosset and Dunlap, 1976.

Liberace, with Shirley MacLaine. *The Wonderful Private World of Liberace*. New York: Harper and Row, 1986.

Thomas, Bob. *Liberace: The True Story*. New York: St. Martin's Press, 1987.

Thorson, Scott, with Alex Thorleifson. *Behind the Candelabra: My Life with Liberace*. New York: Dutton, 1988.

CHRONOLOGY

1919 Born Wladziu Valentino Liberace in West Allis, Wisconsin, on May 16

1926 Meets the world-famous concert pianist and performer Ignacy Jan Paderewski

1933 First public performance, at a speakeasy in Milwaukee

1939 Invited to play with the Chicago Symphony in its Milwaukee appearance; receives first newspaper review; takes on stage name Walter Buster Keys

1940 Leaves Wisconsin for New York City; starts using Liberace as a stage name

1942 Leaves New York for Los Angeles; lives with Clarence Goodwin for over a year

1945 Hired by the Last Frontier Hotel in Las Vegas; brother George becomes manager

1949 Performs a White House concert; buys first of many houses; invites mother, Frances Zuchowski Liberace, to live with him; reads and is deeply influenced by Claude Bristol's *The Magic of Believing;* appears in first movie, *South Sea Sinner,* opposite Shelley Winters

1950 Liberace first appears on television, eventually getting his own syndicated half-hour TV show

1952 Liberace's show reaches 45 million people weekly over 180 stations

1953 Liberace sets attendance record at the Hollywood Bowl; appears at Carnegie Hall in New York; announces engagement to marry Joanne Rio

1954 Liberace opens the Riviera Hotel in Las Vegas at a salary of $50,000 a week, a new record; lands a starring role in a major Hollywood movie called

Sincerely Yours; visits Rome and is granted a private audience with Pope Pius XII

1956	Liberace performs in London at the invitation of the queen of England; wins $22,400 libel judgment against the *London Daily Mirror*
1957	Breaks with brother George; younger brother Rudy is found dead in a Los Angeles motel room; Liberace's mother is attacked at one of his houses
1963	Almost dies from uremic poisoning caused by a cleaning fluid used on a jacket
1973	Co-authors *Liberace: An Autobiography* with Carroll Carroll; conducts an interview entitled "I Am Not a Homosexual, Says Liberace"
1977	Liberace's estranged father, Salvatore Liberace, dies on April 30; Liberace meets Scott Thorson
1980	Liberace's mother dies; Liberace draws up formal adoption papers that would make Thorson his legal son but never signs them
1982	Liberace breaks with Thorson; Thorson files a lawsuit seeking $113 million
1984	Liberace performs 14 sold-out performances at Radio City Music Hall in New York
1985	Performs 21 sold-out performances at Radio City Music Hall; brother George dies on March 9
1986	Makes final public appearances at Radio City Music Hall; settles lawsuit with Thorson
1987	Signs last will and testament; enters the Eisenhower Medical Center in Palm Springs, California; dies from AIDS on February 4

INDEX

Ray Mungo, a graduate of Boston University, founded the Liberation News Service, an underground press service of the 1960s. The author of numerous books, including *Famous Long Ago* and *Palm Springs Babylon,* Mungo received a Pulitzer Prize nomination for *Total Loss Farm,* a novel that has been in print since 1970. Mungo currently lives in San Diego with his committed partner of 13 years.

Martin Duberman is Distinguished Professor of History at the Graduate Center for the City University of New York and the founder and director of the Center for Lesbian and Gay Studies. One of the country's foremost historians, he is the author of 15 books and numerous articles and essays. He has won the Bancroft Prize for *Charles Francis Adams* ; two Lambda awards for *Hidden from History: Reclaiming the Gay and Lesbian Past,* an anthology that he coedited; and a special award from the National Academy of Arts and Letters for his overall "contributions to literature." His play *In White America* won the Vernon Rice/Drama Desk Award in 1964. His other works include *James Russell Lowell* (1966), *Black Mountain: An Exploration in Community* (1972), *Paul Robeson* (1989), *Cures: A Gay Man's Odyssey* (1991), and *Stonewall* (1993).

Professor Duberman received his Ph.D. in history from Harvard University in 1957 and served as professor of history at Yale University and Princeton University from 1957 until 1972, when he assumed his present position at the City University of New York.